TRADERPSYCHE:
FROM
BIAS
TO
BREAKTHROUGH
REWIRE YOUR MIND. TRANSFORM YOUR TRADING.

ANAND SIVA KUMAR

Chennai • Bangalore

CLEVER FOX PUBLISHING
Chennai, India

Published by CLEVER FOX PUBLISHING 2025
Copyright © Anand Siva Kumar 2025

All Rights Reserved.
ISBN: 978-93-6707-399-5

This book has been published with all reasonable efforts taken to make the material error-free after the consent of the author. No part of this book shall be used, reproduced in any manner whatsoever without written permission from the author, except in the case of brief quotations embodied in critical articles and reviews.

The Author of this book is solely responsible and liable for its content including but not limited to the views, representations, descriptions, statements, information, opinions and references ["Content"]. The Content of this book shall not constitute or be construed or deemed to reflect the opinion or expression of the Publisher or Editor. Neither the Publisher nor Editor endorse or approve the Content of this book or guarantee the reliability, accuracy or completeness of the Content published herein and do not make any representations or warranties of any kind, express or implied, including but not limited to the implied warranties of merchantability, fitness for a particular purpose. The Publisher and Editor shall not be liable whatsoever for any errors, omissions, whether such errors or omissions result from negligence, accident, or any other cause or claims for loss or damages of any kind, including without limitation, indirect or consequential loss or damage arising out of use, inability to use, or about the reliability, accuracy or sufficiency of the information contained in this book.

Disclaimer

This book is intended for educational and informational purposes only.

Trading and investing involve substantial financial risk, and past performance does not guarantee future results.

The psychological strategies, tools, and concepts discussed here reflect the personal experiences and perspectives of the author and are not a substitute for professional financial advice, therapy, or psychiatric treatment.

Readers are solely responsible for their trading decisions and psychological well-being.

Consult a qualified financial advisor, psychologist, or therapist before making significant decisions.

The author, publisher, and any affiliates disclaim any liability for any loss or risk incurred as a consequence of the use and application, directly or indirectly, of any information contained in this book.

"TraderPsyche is the missing piece in every trader's toolkit."

— Meetesh Goyal, Trading Manager.

REWIRE YOUR MIND
TRANSFORM YOUR TRADING

ANAND SIVA KUMAR

Dedication

To Amma,

for her unwavering love, prayers, and silent strength – the foundation beneath every step of my journey.

To Ritu,

for standing beside me through every storm, believing in my growth even when I struggled to believe in myself.

To Dr. Aaron Beck and Dr. Albert Ellis,

whose pioneering work in understanding the mind has given countless individuals, including me, a path toward greater clarity, emotional resilience, and personal transformation.

And to every trader fighting silent battles of the mind, may you find your strength, your clarity, and your victory.

PRAISE FOR TRADERPSYCHE

"TraderPsyche, rarely does a book distil years of experience with such brutal honesty, bringing structure to the mental process of trading, exploring its fallacies, biases, while providing self-experienced solutions." – Venkatesh Pai, VP Commercial, OQ8

"I first met Anand when we both were at Reliance, and I remember him as an ardent fan of technical analysis. So, to see him write TraderPsyche was a pleasant surprise. Anand used his personal trading experiences and learnings of a psychologist, and beautifully brings out what goes inside a trader's head before, during, and after a trade. Simple exercises to help you understand your emotions and how to manage them while trading will help the readers become a better version of themselves. I recommend the book to anyone who is getting into trading or is looking to channelize their emotions better while trading. "– Abhishek Modi, CMT & Professional Trader

"Honest, practical, powerful. TraderPsyche fills the missing gap in most traders, fixing the mind that trades the market." – Amit Daga, Trader, Freepoint Commodities

"Anand has written this engaging book from his life experience. I was amazed at how TraderPsyche resonated with me in my field of expertise, the business of Design. This book is a must-read for not just traders but also for all those trying to understand the puzzle of the mind." – Nima VN, Founder & Design Director at N7 Design & Trading QFZ LLC

Praise for TraderPsyche

"TraderPsyche is a must-read for anyone starting in trading or struggling to understand why their trades aren't working. Anand, from his own life experiences, has written the book highlighting the psychology of a trader, giving a 360-degree view. The powerful combination of practical experiences along with the impact of mindset and emotional reasoning makes it a one-of-a-kind book related to trading and a must-read." - Abdul Harris, Ex Derivatives Trader at NOC.

"TraderPsyche is the missing piece in every trader's toolkit. This book doesn't teach you how to trade, but it teaches you how to think. TraderPsyche dives into the hidden cognitive biases that quietly undermine performance, from overconfidence to fear of missing out. What I appreciated most was how practical the insights were to develop emotional resilience and sharpen decision-making. Highly recommended for anyone serious about long-term success in the markets." – Meetesh Goyal, Trading Manager.

"The role of cortisol and testosterone is the most underrated topic in the trading lifespan of a financial markets trader. TraderPsyche strikes the right chord, prompting readers to synthesize the much-needed balance to make the best of their analytical thinking." – Sudheesh Nambiath, Manager, DMCC, UAE.

CONTENTS

Praise for TraderPsyche — v

Section 1: Understanding the Trader's Mind — ix

Preface — xi
Before You Begin — xv
Trader Self-Reflection Quiz — xvii
Introduction: The Real Battle is Inside — xix

1. The Psychological Battlefield of Trading — 1
2. The Anatomy of a Trading Decision — 6

Section 2: Building Your Mental Foundation — 15

3. Mastering The Mind: My Journey with Cognitive Behavioral Therapy (CBT) and Rational Emotive Behavior Therapy (REBT) — 16

Section 3: Mastering Cognitive Biases and Cognitive Distortions — 30

4. Loss Aversion - The Bias That Holds You Back — 33
5. Overconfidence Bias – When Winning Makes You Weak — 40
6. Confirmation Bias – Seeing What You Want to See — 47
7. Anchoring Bias – The Danger of Getting Stuck — 53
8. Recency Bias – Trapped in the Last Trade — 59
9. The Gambler's Fallacy – Due for a Win? Or Due for a Mistake? — 65

10. The Endowment Effect – Falling in Love with Your Trades — 71
11. The Quiet Biases that keep You Stuck - Sunk Cost Fallacy and Herd Mentality (Reader Reflection Exercise) — 77

Section 4: Mastering Cognitive Distortions — 81

12. Transitioning from Traps to Truth – Moving Inward — 82
13. The Invisible Narrator – Understanding Cognitive Distortions in Trading — 85
14. Catastrophizing – When One Loss Feels Like the End — 89
15. All-or-Nothing Thinking – "If I am Not Winning Everything, I am a Failure" — 95
16. Emotional Reasoning – When Feelings Pretend as Facts — 100
17. Overgeneralization – When One Loss Becomes a Life Pattern — 106
18. Labeling – When One Mistake Defines Who You Are — 109
19. The Journey We Just Took — 112

Section 5: Strengthening the Trader Psyche — 115

20. Trader's Mental Toolbox – Building Your Inner Edge — 116
21. Trader's Behavioral Toolbox – Build Habits that Hold — 123
22. The 90-Day Mental Fitness Plan – One Stage at a Time — 127
23. My 90-Day Transformation: A Personal Journey — 132
24. Mistakes I Made While Fixing My Trading Psychology — 138
25. Conclusion: Mastering Your Trading Psychology — 143

Section 6: Bonus Section — 147

26. TraderPsyche Self-Transformation Mini Workbook — 148

Acknowledgements — *159*
About the Author — *161*
Further Reading and References — *163*

SECTION 1
UNDERSTANDING THE TRADER'S MIND

PREFACE

Trading is often portrayed as a game of numbers, charts, and rapid decisions.

But anyone who has spent years in the markets knows the truth: **it's a game played within the mind.**

My journey into trading began over sixteen years ago, navigating the volatile waters of **Crude Oil, Indian equities,** and **Futures & Options (F&O)** markets. I had the privilege of holding leadership roles in **Trading and Risk Management** at **Reliance Industries Limited** and **Essar Oil UK Limited,** managing Flat Price and Options trading portfolios.

Along the way, I pursued professional certifications, earning the titles of **Chartered Market Technician (CMT), Energy Risk Professional (ERP), and Executive Programme in Algorithmic Trading (EPAT).**

From the outside, trading might seem like a structured, disciplined career path.

But behind the scenes, my trading journey was anything but smooth.

I have lost more money than I can count, made nearly every mistake a trader can make – from emotional revenge trading, to chasing losses, to letting ego blind me to clear market signals.

These painful experiences, more than any textbook or certification, taught me a vital truth: **mastery over the markets begins with mastery over oneself.**

Preface

I still remember the day I was introduced to Technical Analysis by **Mr. Yeshwant Rao** in a brief three-hour session back in 2009.

I was instantly fascinated by the colorful lines, candlesticks, bars, and indicators dancing on the screen.

Immediately after the session, I ran outside, called my wife, and excitedly told her:

"I have stumbled upon something incredible! We're going to make tons of money!"

I didn't realize then that **my mind was already playing games with me**.

Both my wife Ritu and I completed our CMT certifications in 2011, and while I continued to passionately pursue trading, she eventually found her passion in education and teaching.

Armed with technical skills and professional success, I thought transitioning to full-time trading after quitting my high-paying job would be easy.

I couldn't have been more wrong. Trading, after all, can be a lonely and introspective profession.

It took another three years of relearning, reflecting, and reshaping my mental models before I truly aligned my trading and investing with my psyche.

As life unfolded, I also faced deeper internal battles.

During this period, I struggled with episodes of **depression** and periods of **crippling anxiety** – challenges that made trading, already a mental battlefield, even harder.

These experiences taught me that the real war wasn't just against market volatility – it was against the storms within.

In my quest to truly understand the mind behind the market, I pursued academics further, transitioning from a **Bachelor's degree in Chemical Engineering** to a **Master's in Clinical Psychology**, and immersed myself in the tools of healing and resilience.

Today, as a **Certified Cognitive Behavioral Therapy (CBT) Practitioner**, I can say with conviction:

The mind can be retrained. Thought patterns can be reshaped. Strength can be rebuilt.

Along this journey, I also discovered the profound power of **Rational Emotive Behavior Therapy (REBT)**, which taught me how rigid, irrational emotional demands could quietly destroy trading performance.

This unique blend of real-world trading scars, cognitive restructuring (CBT), and emotional rationalization (REBT) gives me a lens through which to see what most traders miss:

It is not market volatility that breaks traders.

It is **cognitive biases**, **irrational beliefs**, and **unchecked emotional patterns**.

This book is born from that realization.

It is not written from a pedestal of perfection, but from the trenches of hard-fought experience, both in the markets and within my mind.

My aim is simple:

To help you identify the invisible psychological traps that sabotage trading performance, and to show you how practical, proven CBT and REBT techniques can be used to overcome them.

If you are willing to look inward – to confront your biases, reshape your beliefs, and strengthen your emotional discipline – you will find in these

Preface

pages a roadmap to not just becoming a better trader, but becoming a master of your own mind.

Welcome to TraderPsyche – where the real trading battle begins.

BEFORE YOU BEGIN

Most trading books focus on the market. This book focuses on you. Before you begin reading, I want to be very clear about what you are about to experience.

This is not a book filled with trading setups, technical patterns, or magical strategies. This is a book about the real fight every trader faces – the mind.

It is about the fears you don't talk about. The greed you can't always control. The emotional storms that destroy even the best trading plans.

You will not be reading passively here. Instead, you will be working, mentally, emotionally, and sometimes painfully, facing your fears and challenging the thoughts that sabotage your growth.

You don't need to be perfect. You do not need to eliminate emotions. You will not be able to actually. You just need to be willing to open up to yourself and look inside honestly, patiently, and consistently.

I have personally used these tools, methods, and exercises many times. They helped me to rebuild myself each time.

If you are ready to stop blaming the market, the news, or the world and start working on the real edge that matters the most, your mind, then you are ready for this journey.

Let us start with a simple reflection.

Before you dive deep into the chapters, take a moment to see what hidden biases and distortions might already be operating inside you.

No judgement. Only honesty, and that is where the real change begins.

TRADER SELF-REFLECTION QUIZ

"Before you start fixing your mind, let's see where the cracks might already be."

— **TraderPsyche**

Instructions:

Read each statement carefully. If it feels like something you have thought, felt, or done during your trading journey, mark it mentally. No judgment, only honest awareness.

Questions:

1. Sometimes I hold onto a losing position just because selling would feel like admitting defeat.
2. After a big loss, a part of me wants to "win back" immediately, no matter what the setup is.
3. I catch myself only searching for news or opinions that agree with the trades I have already taken.
4. If my strategy hits two to three losses in a row, I start doubting whether it even works.
5. I often tell myself, "Because I lost today, tomorrow will probably be bad too."

6. Even when my plan says exit, I hesitate, hoping the trade will magically turn.
7. I have blamed the market, brokers, or external factors many times to feel better after a bad outcome.
8. I find it easier to act on a trade idea if everyone else on social media seems excited about it.
9. I often think, "If I am not winning big, I am failing. There is no in between."
10. After a few good trades, I feel almost invincible and start taking bigger risks than planned.

How to use this (small) quiz?

- If 3 or more statements resonate with you or feel true: **Congratulations**, you are already self-aware.
- As you read this book, you will find out **why** you do these things and **how** to rebuild your mind around them.
- You are not alone. Every trader who ever grew strong had to walk through these emotional storms first.

INTRODUCTION:
THE REAL BATTLE IS INSIDE

"Let me begin with clarity:
This book is for market participants of any asset class"

- Those who are consistently making losses in the markets.
- Those who are unable to make consistent profits over time.
- Those who are unsure why they are even in the markets.
- Those who dream of buying a Range Rover or BMW after taking a huge risk on a single trade.
- Those who find themselves praying for their positions just to reach breakeven, just to escape.
- Those who take out the frustrations of life on the market.
- Who believe they are destined to lose and somewhere deep down, are strangely comfortable with it.
- Who are new to trading and do not want to experience all the costly mistakes and learn.
- Those who are at times successful in markets but in between commit mistakes which dent their performance big time.

The list could go on.

If you recognize yourself in any of the above, then this book is for you. Please read ahead.

When people consider what makes a trader successful, they often think about things like technical analysis, managing risk, and understanding financial terms. Rarely, if ever, does anyone talk about the battlefield that matters the most:

The trader's mind.

If you have been trading for any length of time, chances are you already know something most books never teach:

Every trade you place is not just a battle against the market – it's a battle against yourself.

A battle against your emotions, your fears, your biases, and your distorted thinking.

Think about it:

- How many times have you entered a trade perfectly, only to exit too early out of fear during a minor pullback?
- How often have you clung to a losing position, hoping and praying it would turn around, ignoring every warning sign?
- How many winning trades have you missed because fear of loss overwhelmed you after a losing streak?
- How big of a position have you taken after a winning streak, driven by overconfidence?

These are not problems of strategy.

They are problems of psychology.

And they are far more common – and far more damaging – than most traders realize.

Trading triggers some of the deepest, most primal emotions a human can feel:

- Fear
- Greed
- Anger
- Hope
- Shame
- Euphoria

But there are even more dangerous, invisible forces at play – ones that most traders are completely unaware of:

- **Cognitive Biases** – mental shortcuts that distort decisions under pressure.
- **Irrational Beliefs** – rigid emotional demands we place on ourselves, like *"I must not lose"* or *"I must always be right."*

These hidden forces quietly damage trading performance, creating endless cycles of frustration, impulsive decisions, self-doubt, and emotional exhaustion.

Yet, most traders continue to chase better systems, better indicators, and better news feeds – while the real enemy operates silently within.

The Good News: You Can Rebuild Your TraderPsyche

Fortunately, there is a path forward,
a way to identify these internal distortions, to challenge them, and to retrain your mind for greater clarity, discipline, and emotional resilience.

This book combines two of the most powerful psychological frameworks available:

- **Cognitive Behavioral Therapy (CBT)** – to help you recognize and restructure distorted thought patterns.
- **Rational Emotive Behavior Therapy (REBT)** – to help you dismantle irrational emotional demands and build rational, reality-accepting beliefs.

And here's something crucial:

You do not need to eliminate emotions to succeed in trading.

You need to understand them, manage them, and refuse to be ruled by them.

If you are tired of blaming the market, blaming the news, blaming luck, and are finally ready to look inside yourself for the real edge, then you have already taken the first step toward true mastery.

What You Will Gain from This Book

Through practical tools, case studies, worksheets, and mental exercises, you will learn how to:

- Spot the invisible cognitive biases derailing your trades.
- Identify and challenge irrational beliefs creating emotional turmoil.
- Apply structured CBT and REBT techniques to build a stronger, calmer trading mind.
- Design your **90-day mental fitness plan** to permanently upgrade your TraderPsyche.

The market doesn't beat you. Your untrained mind does.

Train your mind – and the markets will start to look very different.

Welcome to **TraderPsyche**.

Your transformation begins now.

CHAPTER 1

THE PSYCHOLOGICAL BATTLEFIELD OF TRADING

"In trading, your mind is not just a tool – it's your first opponent."

— **TraderPsyche**

1.1 The Illusion of Control

Like every person who ventures into trading, I too entered the world of trading believing that success would be a matter of learning strategies, technical setups, and financial models.

Candle stick patterns, moving averages, risk reward ratios, waves, indicators, all seemed like a clean, logical game.

In the beginning, there is a sense of excitement and optimism: "If I master the charts, I will master the markets."

Winning in trading is not only about spotting patterns in the market. It also requires understanding and managing your own emotions and reactions. Overcoming the chaos within yourself is key to success.

No matter how much you prepare technically, you soon realize the real war is being fought inside your mind.

1.2 Trading unleashes primitive emotions

Trading is not like most professions. Nowhere else are you exposed daily to very high uncertainty, risk, loss, greed, and fear. These are the most primal emotions, and they served our ancestors well to survive in the wild. But today, sitting in the comfort of an office or home, they are disastrous when unleashed without control in the modern markets.

In a split second, a trader can move from logical thinking to emotional chaos:

- A small loss feels like a personal failure.
- A sudden profit feels like invincibility.
- A losing streak triggers desperation.
- A winning streak triggers reckless overconfidence.

And all of this happens before you realize what's happening inside you.

1.3 Why the mind becomes the First Enemy

The problem is not that traders feel emotions. The problem is that they are often unaware of how deeply these emotions are affecting their decisions.

Without awareness and training, your mind:

- Amplifies losses emotionally beyond their real financial impact.
- Suppresses risk when greed takes over.
- Distorts judgment through hidden cognitive biases.
- Creates irrational beliefs that sabotage discipline.

You are not just trading markets; you are constantly trading against your psychological reactions. Each time you buy or sell, your emotions, biases, and belief systems are secretly whispering, shouting, or pulling at you.

And if you cannot recognize and manage them, they will for sure defeat you, even if your technical analysis is flawless.

1.4 Cognitive Biases – The silent killers of trading performance

I learned about Cognitive biases in detail when I was learning about Cognitive Behavioral Therapy. These biases distort your perception of reality. A few examples would be

- Overconfidence Bias tricks you into risking too much.
- Loss Aversion locks you into losing trades.
- Confirmation Bias blinds you to warning signs.
- Recency Bias makes you overvalue the most recent market moves.

There are many more, and we will go through them in detail, and methods to overcome them too.

1.5 The Double-Edged Sword: Freedom and Responsibility

In trading, you are alone with your decisions. There is no boss giving orders, no office politics, no customers to please.

This freedom is exhilarating, right? WRONG it's many times terrifying.

Because every success, every failure, every missed opportunity, it all comes back to you.

I realized this in 2019 when I became full-time trader. The initial months were very exciting, and the feeling of freedom was fantastic. Slowly, my discipline started wavering, my biases started creeping in, my risk management was off, and one fine day, I had my biggest loss-making trade, which almost broke me. Had it been a professional setup with someone to report on, my discipline, risk management, and trade quality would have been much better.

Trading forces, you to confront who you are – your strengths, your weaknesses, your fears, your fantasies, and illusions.

Few other professions strip away external excuses so brutally. Few other professions demand such relentless self-awareness and self-mastery.

1.6 The Call to Arms: Prepare your mind, not just your charts

If you want to succeed in trading long term, you must approach it for what it is:

A daily psychological battle where the enemy is within.

This is especially true for every discretionary trader and investor, but also important for a system trader.

You must learn to:

- Identify your emotional triggers.
- Recognize your cognitive biases.
- Challenge your irrational beliefs.
- Train your mind for clarity, resilience, and discipline.

This book is your guide on that inner battlefield. We will explore the hidden traps of trader psychology and, more importantly, we will arm you with the tools to navigate them.

While technical mastery can make you good, mental mastery is what will make you last.

Welcome to the true battlefield. Your mind is the terrain. Your thoughts are the weapons. Your emotional discipline is your armor.

It's time to begin.

Reflection questions

1. When was the last time you made a trading decision that you later realized was driven by emotion rather than logic? Describe what happened, what emotion was strongest, and how it affected your result.
2. Which emotion tends to dominate your trading during high-pressure situations – fear, greed, frustration, hope, or overconfidence? Be honest. No emotion is bad – recognizing the dominant one is the first step.
3. Think of one major trading mistake you recently made. Was it because of a cognitive bias like Overconfidence, Loss Aversion, or Confirmation Bias? Which bias do you think influenced you the most?
4. Do you find it harder to accept losses or to manage your emotions after a string of wins? Why? Understanding which phase triggers more irrational behavior can reveal your deeper vulnerabilities.
5. On a scale of 1 to 10, how much attention have you honestly given to training your mindset and emotions compared to learning technical or fundamental trading skills? Should you rebalance your focus?

CHAPTER 2

THE ANATOMY OF A TRADING DECISION

> *"Don't worry about what the markets are going to do, worry about what you are going to do in response to the markets"*
>
> **– Jack Schwager**

2.1 The Illusion of Rationality

Ask any trader after a losing streak why things went wrong, and you will hear about bad luck, bad setups, or bad timing.

Rarely will you hear about what happened.

- Emotional hijack
- Cognitive bias
- Distorted interpretation

The truth is that trading decisions, especially in discretionary trading, are rarely pure acts of logic. They are complex emotional responses, layered with hope, fear, excitement, and hidden mental traps.

I have hesitated to cut a losing trade and have made it to a mammoth loss, have started a trade as a swing trade and have become a long-term investor, felt euphoric after a winning trade and doubled my position size in the next. Many of you will relate to this. At the moment of taking the trade and being in the trade, all rational thoughts sometimes cease to exist.

Let us explore the 5 stages of every trading decision where things can go wrong.

2.2 The five invisible stages of every trading decision

Every time you place a trade, a psychological journey unfolds – mostly beneath the surface. Let's go through the five stages.

Stage 1: Perception – Seeing the setup

I read the news every morning, check my watchlists from the previous day, and scan the charts. Suddenly, something "looks good". A pattern catches the eye. An opportunity seems obvious.

But perception is never neutral. What you notice and what you ignore is already being filtered through:

- Your recent experiences (Recency Bias)
- Your hopes and fears (Motivated Perception)
- Your emotional state (After a big win or loss)

Many times, in this stage, we don't see things as they are, we see things as we are.

I can recall a perfect setup I spotted, only to realize later that I was emotionally projecting my success into it. This happens to me mostly after a series of wins, where overconfidence sets in and discipline goes for a toss.

Stage 2: Emotional Activation – Feeling the urge

How many of you, after finding the stocks and being ready with all setups, find their body showing signs of heart racing, palms sweating, and a surge of excitement (greed) or dread(fear).

These automatic emotional responses prime you toward quick action and make you careless.

You feel the urgency:

"If I don't act now, I'll miss out."

"If I don't close now, I'll lose everything."

As a trader, I realized later in my trading journey that I have a slight bias towards going short at tops than going long at bottoms. This was because the short trades generally tend to make great returns within a short period of time. This made me jump into trades with the feeling of "If I don't act now, I'll miss out ".

Have you ever rushed into a trade just to relieve the tension inside you?

Stage 3: Interpretation – Telling yourself a story

The mind loves stories.

You start explaining to yourself why this trade makes sense:

- Last time, this setup worked perfectly.
- This time will be different.
- I need to recover losses from earlier.

At this stage, hidden irrational beliefs drive the narrative:

- "I must not lose."
- "If I win this trade, I'll prove I am good enough."
- "Missing this move would be unbearable."

I used to connect my worth with the wins in Trading. I used to be emotionally attached to my salary after leaving my job. The sense of security that a salary brings is not there in trading, and to anticipate it was wrong. My irrational belief was "I need a fixed salary every month from trading". This made me sell options for higher premiums and take unnecessary risks.

Have you ever convinced yourself to enter or hold on to a trade even when clear warning signs were present, simply because you needed it to work?

Stage 4: Decision Formation – Choosing under pressure

Finally, logic, emotions, biases, and stories blend into a decision: Buy, Sell, Hold, Exit.

But if earlier stages were contaminated with irrational thoughts and biases, this decision is already compromised, even if it feels rational.

Sometimes hesitation creeps in. Sometimes impulsivity takes over. Sometimes we abandon our trading plan completely, without even realizing it.

This stage is greatly affected by other stages, and let me explain with an example.

I heard the news overnight, affecting the overall market and the US, European equity markets were all down significantly. I anticipated a major fall in every stock, and my mind made the mistakes mentioned in Steps 1 to 3. By the next day, market opening, I was charged with emotions and was waiting for the market to open and go short. I started shorting the index, the market went in my way, and I searched for the losers of the day and started shorting them one by one, and soon went way out of my position sizing. My mind was only focusing on the big profits I was about to make, and I had fully lost focus on the risk part.

Have you ever taken a trade so quickly that you barely remember the reasoning afterward?

Stage 5: Execution and Emotional Reinforcement

Taking the trade is just the start of the emotional storm. It intensifies:

- Relief if the price moves in your favor.
- Panic if it moves against you.

And depending on the result, you internalize new "lessons"- often wrong ones:

- Overconfidence after a random win ("I am invincible", "I am destined for trading glory", "what will I do with all the profits?")
- Learned helplessness after a loss ("I can't win no matter what", "I am a loser", "I will never be successful", "I deserve this.")

These emotional shocks shape future trades, deepening emotional habits both good and bad.

Coming back to our short position taken in the previous step. After showing initial profits, the market turns back up fast, and now I am unable to get out of the positions as my mind is still producing dopamine from the profits which was made (in my daydreams). And finally, I stopped out when the pain was too large to bear anymore.

Have you ever gotten reckless after a big win or frozen with fear after a big loss?

Stages of Trading Decision

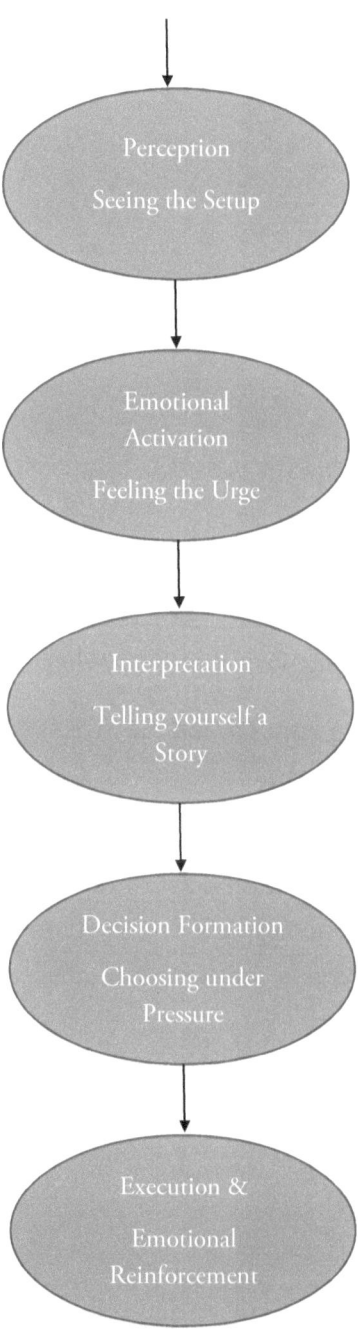

2.3 Why most traders stay stuck

Most traders never slow down enough to examine this process. They remain trapped in an endless cycle of

- Emotional reactions
- Biased perceptions
- Irrational beliefs
- Random decisions
- Reinforced emotional patterns.

They change indicators, they chase new strategies. They blame markets, brokers, or the news.

But they never realize that the real cycle begins inside their mind.

2.4 The Hidden Truth

"You are not trading the market. You are trading your interpretation of the market, filtered through emotion and belief."

Until you put in efforts to understand the invisible emotional architecture behind every trade, no amount of technical skill can consistently save you.

In the next sections, we will learn how concepts of psychology – especially Cognitive Behavioral Therapy (CBT) and Rational Emotive Behavioral Therapy (REBT), give us a tool to catch, challenge, and change these hidden distortions at their root.

"Mastering the markets begins with mastering the mirror.

The real chart you must read first is the one inside your mind."

Mini-Exercise:

"Mapping Your Last 5 Trades"

- Think back to your last five trades (whether winning or losing).
- For each trade, ask yourself:

Question	Reflection
At Stage 1 (Perception):	Did I objectively spot the setup, or was I emotionally biased?
At Stage 2 (Emotional Activation):	What emotions did I feel before entering? Fear, greed, urgency?
At Stage 3 (Interpretation):	What inner story or belief influenced my action?
At Stage 4 (Decision Formation):	Did I act according to a plan or impulse?
At Stage 5 (Execution/ Feedback):	How did I emotionally react after the outcome? Overconfidence? Fear? Despair?

Why this exercise matters:

Awareness always comes before change. Before you can improve your trading decisions, you must first understand how they are currently being made.

Write your thoughts here

Question	Reflection
At Stage 1 (Perception):	
At Stage 2 (Emotional Activation):	
At Stage 3 (Interpretation):	
At Stage 4 (Decision Formation):	
At Stage 5 (Execution/Feedback):	

SECTION 2
BUILDING YOUR MENTAL FOUNDATION

CHAPTER

3

MASTERING THE MIND: MY JOURNEY WITH CBT AND REBT

"Markets are uncertain. Your mind doesn't need to be"

— TraderPsyche

3.1 My introduction to CBT and REBT

The majority of trading books suggest following a plan, using risk management and position sizing, and then if you use any strategy with a slight edge, you will succeed. This is the general pattern. Now tell me, when everyone knows this then why only less than 1% of traders succeed? Why are the majority of us not able to follow our plan, follow risk management, follow proper position sizing, and jump from one strategy to another?

I sought strategies, indicators, and reliable market setups. Yet, despite mastering Candlestick patterns, Indicators, Elliott waves, and Risk management, the emotional rollercoaster never stopped.

- I would enter perfect setups only to exit too early out of fear.
- I would hold on to losers longer than planned, hoping and praying.

- I would break my trading plan by increasing the position sizing and then go and check a very low time frame, like 3-minute charts, to look for some bias towards my direction.

It was confusing for me. Even after getting the best certification in technical analysis and risk management, why was my execution still so broken?

3.2 Discovering the tools to fight back

I was introduced to Cognitive Behavior Therapy (CBT) and Rational Emotive Behavior Therapy(REBT) as part of my therapy sessions for depression and anxiety. These were life-changing for me in terms of health, and both the above frameworks were designed to help people with anxiety, depression, and emotional disorders.

I knew deep down my trading problems weren't about knowledge or purpose – they were emotional. The struggles were all related to how I thought about the markets, how I reacted internally, and what irrational beliefs and biases I unknowingly carried.

This discovery has been a turning point in my trading journey.

3.3 What is Cognitive Behavioral Therapy (CBT)?

Cognitive Behavioral Therapy, or CBT, developed by Dr. Aaron T Beck in the 1960s, is a psychological approach based on a very simple idea:

"Our thoughts shape our emotions, and our emotions shape our behaviors."

In CBT, the focus is on the connection between:

- What you think (your inner dialogue)
- How you feel (your emotional reactions)
- How you act (your behavior in the world)

In trading terms, this can be:

- A market event (like a loss or sudden, volatile movement in the market) triggers an automatic thought.
- The thought causes an emotional reaction, like fear of missing out or fear of losing everything.
- That emotion drives trading behavior, mostly impulsive or irrational.

CBT helps us to identify the faulty or distorted thoughts, challenge their truth, and replace them with healthier, rational explanations.

Over time, this reduces emotional overreactions and builds more consistent behavior, which is exactly what traders need.

3.4 The Cognitive Triad: How Traders Get Stuck

One of the fundamental concepts developed by Dr Aaron Beck, the father of CBT, is the Cognitive Triad. It explains how a person can have distorted thinking in three key areas.

1. **View of Self – How you see yourself** – "I am a terrible trader", "I am not fit for doing anything".
2. **View of the World(Markets)** – How you see the external world – "The market is rigged against me", "Big players are the only ones who win in trading", "You need sophisticated software to be profitable in trading and investment".
3. **View of the Future** – How you see your future, the possibilities and hope – "I will never succeed as a trader", "The stock reverses the moment I get into trading".

When one or more of the three areas become negative, it leads to feelings of hopelessness, frustration, and giving up, and it destroys trading discipline.

Let me share a real-life example with you: I went through a major losing streak, and my thinking patterns were like below.

- **View of Self: You start thinking**
  "I am not fit for becoming a trader", "I am stupid to have left my job for trading".

- **View of Markets(World): You start believing**
  "Markets are random and manipulative", "Nothing works", "People will start thinking of me as a loser".

- **View of the Future: You conclude**
  "I will never be a successful trader", "This field is not for me", "I am not good at anything", "There is no point in trying anymore".

Notice how a simple losing streak has triggered a full collapse across the Cognitive Triad. This negative spiral often leads to abandoning trading plans, revenge trading, or quitting trading altogether out of despair.

3.5 How CBT helps break the Triad

CBT teaches you to

1. Catch these negative patterns early,
2. Challenge the distortions logically,
3. Reframe the narrative to something more rational and empowering.

Taking the previous example, instead of

- I am not fit for becoming a trader; you replace it with: "I made mistakes, but I can learn, adapt, and improve like everyone else."
- Markets are random and manipulative; you replace it with: "Markets are neutral. Many traders and investors have been profitable. It's my skill, preparation, and emotional resilience that matter."

- I will never be a successful trader; you replace it with: "Success is built over time through consistent small improvements, not overnight wins".

Correcting the triad restores emotional balance and reignites motivation, allowing you to trade rationally, consistently, and sustainably again.

3.6 What I Learned from Cognitive Behavioral Therapy (CBT)

When I first encountered CBT, it felt like someone was finally describing what was happening inside me and in clear, logical terms. I realized that every time I faced trading setbacks, a chain reaction would happen automatically, with my thought patterns changing towards being harsh and critical, blaming markets, and feeling hopeless about my future in trading.

CBT taught me that these negative thought spirals were not facts, but they were my interpretations, and interpretations could be:

- Observed
- Questioned
- Changed.

I started applying simple but powerful CBT questions to my trading reflections:

- Is this thought 100% true? To challenge distortions
- Am I exaggerating the outcome – To catch cognitive errors
- What is the evidence for and against the belief – To bring logical balance
- What would I tell a friend in the same situation – To soften harsh self-judgment

Slowly, the mental patterns began to break and

- A loss was just a loss – not a statement about my worth.
- The market was just a system, not an enemy plotting against me.
- The future was still open, and every day was a new opportunity to improve.

Trading still didn't come easily, but it became less self-destructive. And that alone changed everything.

3.7 CBT Reflection Worksheet: Catch your thought traps

Reflect on a recent trade where you felt strong emotions (fear, anger, excitement, shame). Fill in the table below honestly.

Step	Your Example
Situation	What happened?(Stop loss hit, missed entry, big win/loss)
Automatic thought	What was your first thought about it? (honest answer please)
Emotion	What feeling did that thought trigger?(fear, anger, sadness, excitement)
Behavior	What did you do immediately afterward?(revenge trade, freeze, overtrade, give up)
Reality Check	Was the thought 100% true or distorted? What is a more rational way to view it?
Replacement thought	Write a healthier, more rational version of the original thought.

An example from my journal

Step	My Example
Situation	Made a series of big wins, and the overall view of the market is coming right.
Automatic thought	This is the time to make the maximum money. Will buy the Range Rover with the profits.
Emotion	Excitement, I cannot wait for the next day, and if it's weekend, then I am in hell.
Behavior	Overtrade, taking high risks in one direction
Reality Check	The thought was 100% distorted as I was not looking at the risk at all. I was overtrading and not following my plan.
Replacement thought	I am happy that I am on a winning streak, but I should follow my plan and should not risk more than what was decided during pre-market hours. My views can be right, and many times they can be dead wrong too. So, I should wait for my setup to trigger and wait patiently for existing trades to be complete to add more risk.

Instructions to reader – Spend 5 to 10 minutes filling this worksheet after trading days where you felt strong emotions (both good and bad days). You will be amazed at how quickly your mind's hidden traps become visible.

1. **Situation**

2. **Automatic thought**

3. **Emotion**

4. **Behavior**

5. **Reality check**

6. **Replacement thought**

3.8 What is Rational Emotive Behavior Therapy (REBT)

While CBT helped me understand and change my automatic negative thoughts, REBT took me even deeper to uncover the deep, irrational beliefs that were shaping my emotions and actions.

REBT was developed by Dr. Albert Ellis in the 1950s. REBT teaches a powerful idea:

"It is not just what happens to you that causes emotional suffering – It is the irrational demands and rigid beliefs that you hold about those events."

In trading terms, it means that

- Losing a trade isn't what destroys you emotionally – It is believing "I must never lose".
- Missing a great trade isn't what triggers despair – It is believing "I must always catch every opportunity or I am a failure".

REBT focuses on uncovering and challenging these hidden "musts", "shoulds" that create extreme emotional reactions.

The goal is to replace extreme irrational demands with rational preferences, making your mind stronger, calmer, and more flexible under pressure.

3.9 My breakthrough with REBT

For a long time in my life and trading journey, I was trapped by invisible emotional rules I had created for myself:

- "I must make money every month or I am failing".
- "My trading view should always be right, or I am incompetent".
- "I should earn as much as possible from trading, else others will think less of me".

- "Since I left my high-paying job for personal trading, I should make more than my salary from trading".
- "My worth is connected to trading income, and people will not respect me even if my other businesses are doing well".
- "I should be able to catch every big move in stocks listed in the Futures & Options section."

The list could go on. Whenever reality violated these rigid beliefs, which it often did because markets are volatile in nature, I would get frustrated, angry, and would be in despair. Finally, I would self-sabotage myself and my equity curve.

REBT opened my eyes to the fact that my emotional breakdowns weren't the result of the market's movements after all. It's been a game-changer in understanding my reactions! They were caused by my irrational demands on how the market should behave, as per my view.

Through REBT, I learned to replace the rigid beliefs with healthier and more realistic ones.

Irrational Belief	Rational Alternative
"I must not lose"	"I prefer to win, but I accept that losses are normal."
"I must always catch the big moves."	"I would like to catch good moves, but missing trades is part of the process."
"Since I left my high-paying job for personal trading, I should make more than my salary from trading."	"There is no relationship between my previously drawn salary and the markets. I would like to make a decent annualized percentage return on the amount invested in my trading portfolio without taking unnecessary risks."

This shift in mindset didn't directly eliminate losses, but it reduced the probability of making an emotional mistake in trading.

It **reduced the emotional devastation that used to follow every setback.**

And that emotional resilience made consistent trading possible.

3.10 The REBT ABCDE model – Simplified for traders

REBT uses a powerful 5-step process called the ABCDE model to structure irrational thinking:

Step	Meaning	Trading Example
A – Activating Event	Something Happens, Trigger	Your stop loss hits
B – Belief	What do you believe about it	"I must never lose"
C – Consequence	The emotional and behavioral reaction	Rage, revenge trades, despair
D – Disputation	Questioning the belief	"Is it true that I must never lose?"
E – Effective New Belief	A more rational belief	"I prefer to win, but I accept losses are part of the game."

Please note that **Event A doesn't cause the emotional pain. It is the irrational belief that causes it.** By disputing the rigid belief, you create a healthier emotional response.

Applying REBT to Trading: A real-life example

I had reduced my portfolio positions as my view on Equities was toppish and I was expecting a deeper correction in markets. Bear markets sometimes have sharper rallies and it will test your conviction.

A – Activating event – A bear market counter trend rally was happening, and stock prices were going up by 2% to 5% for the day.

B – Belief – "I shouldn't miss any big moves in the market. If I am not fully invested, I will miss the next big rally".

C – Consequence – I started buying the stocks which was on my radar and ended up spending my entire capital in a single day. I forgot that I had a plan to add 20% stocks on corrections of every x%.

D – Disputation – I started to question my belief by asking the following questions. "Is it true that if I miss this rally market will never correct to give me another chance?". "How many times in my past have I been able to catch the exact bottom?". "Why is this time different?". "How will I feel when I have invested all the money at current levels and the market corrects further below?".

E – Effective new belief – I changed my irrational belief of "I should not miss any big moves in the market" to "No one can catch every big move in the market. I am participating by buying good stocks on corrections and at better valuations". "Markets will give me enough chances to make money even if I miss a few chances."

By doing this, instead of spiraling emotionally, you stay rational, patient, and ready for the next setup.

REBT reflection worksheet: Changing your Trading beliefs

Pick one recent trading event that triggered a strong negative emotion.

Fill in the REBT template.

Step	Your Example
A – Activating Event	What happened? (big loss, missed trade)
B – Irrational Belief	What rigid belief did you hold about it? ("I must not lose", "I should always be right")
C – Emotional Consequence	What emotion and action did this belief cause? (anger, despair, overtrading)
D – Disputation	How would you challenge this belief logically? ("Is it realistic? Is it helpful?")
E – Effective New Belief	What rational belief can you adopt instead? ("Losses are uncomfortable but tolerable")

Step	Your Example
A – Activating Event	
B – Irrational Belief	
C – Emotional Consequence	
D – Disputation	
E – Effective New Belief	

SECTION 3
MASTERING COGNITIVE BIASES AND COGNITIVE DISTORTIONS

"Trade what you see, not what you think"

– **Anonymous**

The Invisible Saboteurs of Trading

As traders, we like to believe we are rational. We build systems, set risk parameters, and use checklists, all to protect ourselves from impulsive decisions.

Yet even the best traders often fall into predictable mental traps – patterns of biased thinking that distort decisions and destroy performance.

They are called Cognitive biases and Cognitive distortions.

- **Cognitive biases** – Automatic mental shortcuts that cause systematic judgment errors.
- **Cognitive distortions** – Irrational thought patterns that exaggerate emotional pain and fear.

Both distort trading. Both must be understood and corrected.

I have spent years building systems, back testing strategies, studying data from different sources, and chasing the "edge". But the "edge" started to stick only when I started to turn inward and tried to examine how my mind was interpreting and reacting to the market.

You can have the best strategy in the world but if your mind is distorted by fear, revenge, perfectionism or false certainty, you will find a way to destroy it. In real trading, the following situation typically manifests: When a trade goes slightly against you, you may refuse to exit, hoping that it will turn around, driven by loss aversion.

These biases and distortions show up in the hesitation to take a trade, in the urge to double down after a win, in the belief that this time will be different.

The hardest part is that you don't realize they are working on you till the damage is done.

In the next few chapters, we are not just defining these biases and distortions. We are going to understand how they are going to show up inside your trades and, more importantly, how you can start catching them before they take control.

I have personally experienced each of these biases, sometimes more than once and often very painfully. However, what matters is that each of them taught me an essential lesson that contributed to my growth as a trader.

In the following chapters, we will go through each major bias and distortion one at a time. You will see what they are, how they show up in trading, what my experience was with them, and how CBT and REBT principles can help you free yourself from their grip.

This is where the real shift happens. You need to stop the emotions from distorting your decisions. Let us begin.

CHAPTER 4

LOSS AVERSION: THE BIAS THAT HOLDS YOU BACK

> *"Loss Aversion isn't just a bias, its your brain screaming louder for survival than for success."*
>
> – anonymous

4.1 The first and most dangerous bias: Loss Aversion

Of all the biases that affect traders, Loss Aversion is one of the most devastating.

Loss aversion is the human tendency to feel the pain of losses more strongly than the pleasure of equivalent gains.

Research shows that losing Rs 100000 feels two to three times more painful than the pleasure of gaining Rs 100000.

In trading terms:

- A Rs 50000 profit feels good.
- A Rs 50000 loss feels catastrophic and far more emotionally intense.

This asymmetry impacts decision-making at every level.

4.2 How loss aversion destroys traders

Here is how Loss Aversion typically manifests in real trading:

Situation	Reaction Driven by Loss Aversion
Trade goes slightly against you	You refuse to exit, hoping it will turn around, because taking a loss feels unbearable.
Trade goes into profit	You rush to book small gains early, afraid that the market will "snatch it away".
After a loss	You hesitate to take the next valid step, afraid of feeling more pain.
After a win	You risk more to make sure that when a loss happens, you have enough profit

Loss Aversion leads to:

- Cutting winners short.
- Letting losers run.
- Emotional paralysis.
- Poor risk–reward ratios.

4.3 My struggles with Loss Aversion

In my trading years, I have fallen for this bias without realizing it.

- I would hesitate to close a losing position because I couldn't emotionally accept the "finality" of the loss.
- I would pray for getting back to breakeven instead of following my stop loss rules.

- Many times, I have watched small manageable losses grow into account-damaging disasters – simply because I couldn't mentally book the loss.

I have seen many professional traders fall into this trap. After a big loss will come the trades in which I will exit the winner too quickly, not because the system told me to, but I was afraid of holding the position, and it turns into a loss.

It took me a long time to realize the real enemy was the distorted emotional weighting my mind gave to losses compared to gains.

4.4 Real-life example from my Trading Career

One memory stands out even today.

- I had entered a long option (Put) position in crude oil in a forward month (Say Dec month and we are now in June) based on technical setup and market flow. This trade is not in MCX and was an over-the-counter trade. Also, the majority of crude oil options were Asian Price options rather than the common American or European.
- Initially, the trade moved slightly against me, and even though my stop loss was pre-defined, I told myself that it's a long option position in a much farther month. There is nothing to worry about and the market always comes back in few weeks or months' time.

The real reason? I was not able to book the loss and I was praying as price kept on moving against me. By the time I exited, option premium had fallen so much that my drawdown was more than three to four times the initial stop loss. It was something which could have been easily controlled if I had acted rationally.

That trade and many more like that taught me a painful truth: "It is not the market that causes deep losses, it's the refusal to accept small ones on time".

Buying a long-dated option and sitting on the position without any hedge or stop loss is a sure-shot way to destroy your account.

What should have been done?

I should have:

- Predefined stop losses and accepted them mentally if not entering in system before entering any trade.
- Using fixed risk per trade (e.g., 1% or 2% of the account) so that losses are never devastating.
- Celebrating disciplined exits, even the losing trades, because they meant I followed my plan.

4.5 How CBT helped me fight loss aversion and follow my plan

CBT helped me see that my reactions were not bad luck and that they were predictable emotional responses based on distorted thinking.

Through CBT, I started practicing:

- Catching Automatic thoughts – "If I take this loss, it means I am a failure", "This trade will be a big winner and fulfill all my dreams. I need to give it a bit more room and time".
- Challenging the thoughts – "Is that true? Even the best traders lose trades daily". "How many times have your convictions about a big trade turned out to be true?".
- Reframing the thoughts – "Taking a loss is not a failure. It is a professional execution of risk management". "My success in achieving

a single large profitable trade is very rare, and considering the small amount of time due to options expiry, the probability of achieving such a trade is very small".

Over time, this shifted my emotional experience of losses from shame to manageable discomfort.

4.6 How REBT helped me build emotional strength

REBT helped me go even deeper and helped me understand that I was going through a bad phase in trading because of the irrational demands I was placing on myself.

A few of them I realized were:

- "I must be profitable every day."
- "My Broker Console P&L should be green every day with no reds in between."
- "Losses are unbearable and I should take my profits soon, else it will again turn into a big loss."
- "A move against my existing positions in profits will wipe away my profits, and I will be in huge loss again."

Through REBT, I disputed and replaced these rigid beliefs.

Irrational Belief	Rational Placement
"I must be profitable every day."	"No one can win every day. I will have winning days and losing days. I will have to follow my plan, and no one is judging whether I am profitable today or not. I need to be profitable through the year and make the best out of the winning trades."

"A move against my existing positions in profits will wipe away all my profits, and I will be in loss again."	"Markets don't move up in a straight line. They are volatile and they correct to supports in every rally. I have followed my plan and I exactly know where to get out if my trade goes wrong. I have not overleveraged myself. I will hold on to my winners until my trailing stop loss is hit or my targets are achieved."

Please understand that there are no right or wrong answers here. What I have given as rational placement is what is right for me. For you, it might be something different. But whatever the sentence is, the concept is to change our irrational thinking pattern to a more positive and rational one.

Another important aspect to remember is to write these thoughts down. The action of writing the thoughts make it easier for your mind to retain it for long time and also to remember it during stressful situations.

4.7 Reflection Exercise: Face your Loss Aversion

Take a moment to reflect on your last 5 big losing trades. Answer honestly:

Question

- Did you hesitate to book your loss? Why?
- What Automatic thoughts arose? ("It will come back", "I cannot afford to lose")
- What rigid belief was driving your emotion? ("This is my winner, I shouldn't cut it", "I must be profitable for others to respect me")
- How could you challenge that belief rationally?
- What rational belief will you adopt for future trades?

The professional trader is not the one who never loses. The professional trader is the one who accepts that trading is a game of wins and losses and moves forward with discipline.

CHAPTER 5

OVERCONFIDENCE BIAS – WHEN WINNING MAKES YOU WEAK

> *"Almost everyone's instinct is to be overconfident and read way too much into a hot or cold streak"*
>
> **– Nate Silver**

5.1 What is Overconfidence Bias?

Over confidence bias is the human tendency to overestimate:
- Our knowledge,
- Our skills,
- Our ability to predict the future,
- And our control over uncertain events.

In trading, overconfidence shows up when:

- You risk too much after a winning streak.
- You ignore your trading plan because you know this time it's different.
- You start to believe you can feel what the market will do next.

While a certain amount of belief is necessary for trading, Overconfidence makes you become careless and lose your discipline. It blinds you to risks, probabilities, and changing market conditions.

5.2 How Overconfidence blows up accounts

Here is how Overconfidence bias plays out:

Situation	Overconfident Reaction
After a series of winning trades	Day dreaming profits, I should increase my position size dramatically to realize my dreams. I cannot go wrong.
Spotting a setup	Skip proper confirmation signals because "this one is obvious and will break out like the past trades."
After some success	Start believing you have the power to predict market directions, and even if there is a move against you, it is just part of a bigger plan. You just need to wait a bit more, and everything will be profitable again.

Overconfidence finally leads to:
- Blown up accounts after hot streaks.
- Ignoring stop losses.
- Trading setups that don't meet your criteria.

5.3 My Struggles with Overconfidence

I struggle to contain this bias as this makes me lose severely, and then I start to have to deal with Loss Aversion. I have been in this cycle many times till I got it right.

I still remember a month were I was up by 20% in my trading portfolio. I started feeling good, my confidence increased, and to make things worse, my next few trades went profitable too. You will soon understand why it made things worse.

I started getting the feeling, which I recognize now – "I can predict the market to the tick."

- I started taking risks multiple times beyond my normal size. At one point, I had positions in Futures & Options, which were leveraged to the extent of my stock portfolio.
- I entered trades without waiting for full confirmations as everything was rallying.
- I ignored all warning signs because I was consumed by the feeling of hitting the jackpot trade and making it big.
- I started making comments to my wife like **"I will make my entire year's salary in this trade. I am able to feel where the market is going clearly."**

The market did what it always does: It humbled me without mercy.

A few bad trades later, my gains were wiped out, and I lost more than what I had initially thought of.

It wasn't just the loss of money that hurt. It was the emotional crash from feeling invincible to feeling stupid and foolish was devastating.

I was pushed to having Loss Aversion Bias, and my next many months would go in overcoming it. This is a vicious cycle. You become overconfident, your discipline goes for a toss, you take high risks, you lose a lot of money, now you are afraid of taking positions and will cut winning trades soon. The cycle will start again when you start winning in a series of trades, and you again land into overconfidence.

5.4 How CBT helped me control Overconfidence

CBT helped me notice the early warning signs of emotional overconfidence. Through CBT exercises, I started asking myself after every winning streak the following:

What are my Automatic Thoughts – "I am on a roll now.", "My predictions always come true.", "This is the trade I was waiting for all this time.", "This trade will make me rich."

Challenge the Thoughts – "Have I started day dreaming?", "How many times in the past have I lost heavily after a series of wins?", "Do my predictions always come true? Don't they go wrong many times?", "When have I made such huge returns in a single trade, and how many times have I done that in my trading career?"

Replace with Rational Thoughts – "Each trade is independent. Past wins don't guarantee future success. I should follow the system and setups, not my emotions."

"I have been most successful when I patiently waited for a trade and followed my system or setup, and took risks as per my predefined strategy. I will continue to do so."

Practicing this mental discipline helped me normalize my emotional state irrespective of winning or losing. It allowed me to respect risk even when I was winning, not just when I was losing.

5.5 How REBT helped me build Rationality and Confidence

REBT also played a crucial role. Through REBT, I realized that my overconfidence often came from irrational internal demands like:

- "I must make the maximum returns in the shortest time to impress myself and others."
- "I should never lose again now that I have proven myself."
- "My self-worth is connected to my trading profits, and others will respect me only when I am a profitable trader."

REBT taught me to dispute these emotional demands:

Irrational Belief	Rational Replacement
"I must make the maximum returns in the shortest time to impress myself and others."	"I have to make consistent returns, and that too when markets are favorable. When markets are not favorable, I should protect my capital. What I do in markets has no relation to what others or what I have to think of myself."
"I should never lose again now that I have proven myself."	"Losses are always part of trading, and there is a good probability that the next trade could be a loss. Increasing risks based on the last few trades is not the right strategy."

"I have special insight now."	"I have the skill to trade markets, and part of that skill is having proper risk management and position sizing. The skills are not confined to trade selection and making the entry."

Reframing my self–talk protected me from emotional roller coasters and allowed me to maintain consistency over time.

5.6 Reflection Exercise: Detect Your Overconfidence Traps
Reflect honestly:

- After how many winning trades do you start feeling invincible?
- What kinds of risky behavior do you notice during your winning streaks?
- What is one irrational belief you tell yourself during periods of overconfidence?
- How could you dispute and replace that belief rationally?
- What new action plan can you set to stay disciplined during winning streaks?

Protecting yourself during winning periods is equally important to protecting yourself during losses.

CHAPTER 6

CONFIRMATION BIAS: SEEING WHAT YOU WANT TO SEE

"Increasingly, we become so secure in our bubbles that we accept only information, whether true or not, that fits our opinions, instead of basing our opinions on the evidence that's out there."

– Barack Obama

6.1 What is Confirmation Bias?

Confirmation Bias is the human tendency to seek, interpret, and remember information that confirms our existing beliefs while ignoring evidence that contradicts them.

In trading, confirmation bias shows up when

- You selectively look for news, indicators, or chart patterns that support our position.
- You completely ignore warning signs that go against your trade.
- You become emotionally attached to being "right", rather than objectively analyzing the situation.

Confirmation Bias blinds traders by making them hold bad trades longer and ignore obvious market changes. Confirmation bias can happen along with Overconfidence bias and Loss Aversion Bias.

6.2 How Confirmation Bias Sabotages Traders

Confirmation bias affects you in the following ways

Situation	Bias-driven reaction
You enter a trade	You start searching for news, tweets, or chart interpretations supporting your decision.
Trade moves against you	Ignoring warning signs, you focus only on the tiny positives and increase your search for similar views by experts.
New data appears	Reject or ignore any information that challenges your position.

The mind becomes a lawyer arguing for your position emotionally, instead of remaining an unbiased trader who objectively looks at facts.

Confirmation bias increases the chances of:

- Holding losing trades too long.
- Missing early exit signals.
- Adding more to wrong trades (averaging down blindly – related to another bias, which we will discuss later).
- Ignoring the changes in market conditions.

6.3 My Struggles with Confirmation Bias

In my trading journey, I have had to deal with Confirmation Bias many times.

Confirmation Bias: Seeing What You Want to See

I would enter a trade based on a setup, and once in the trade, I would search for reasons and support in terms of expert views on Twitter or comments on websites related to trading to believe my trade was perfect.

Even when the market gave clear signs against my position – a trend reversal or a news shock, I would ignore those warnings.

I remember once being long Crude Oil at the money call options, and I was expecting Crude Oil prices to go up. Once I was in the trade, I started searching for bullish reports by large traders and analysts. There was a very bearish inventory report that was released from the US, and crude reacted and hit my stop loss the same day. I still kept on my position and was frantically searching and hoping for more oversold indicator values, bullish analyst views, bullish technical views, etc.

I was consistently searching for information that supported my view and bias. I was telling myself, "The market is wrong; it will come back." It didn't, and my calls were sold back almost worthless.

In trading, the need to be right is more dangerous than being wrong.

A question for you – Have you taken a large position in say Equities or Equity Index and then, when things started to go wrong, have you logged in to Twitter to see experts who are favoring your side of the view and commented there positively. Have you gone to the Twitter feeds of experts who are in the opposite side of your view and commented there that they know nothing about markets? I have seen people do it and have done it myself once or twice in my trading life, and I consider that moment to be the height of Confirmation bias.

If that feeling is coming to you now, just cut the position, please. You will be in deep trouble soon, as your emotional control is not proper at all.

6.4 How CBT helped me challenge Confirmation Bias

CBT helped me realize that Confirmation Bias was fueled by distorted thought patterns like

- "I need to find as many views that match my position."
- "My analysis must always be correct."

Through CBT exercises, I started practicing:

Catching Automatic Thoughts: "This news/article/analyst view proves my trade is correct."

Challenging the Thoughts: "Am I selectively seeking information? Am I also looking at counter–evidence?"

Reframing the Mindset: "My job is to take the best trade with proper risk management.", "My job is to trade reality as it happens."

I also built a habit: Before taking every major decision, I forced myself to find at least one strong reason why my trade could fail. I also reduced browsing through Twitter and other platforms seeking validating information. This mental discipline helped me reduce the damage caused by Confirmation Bias.

6.5 How REBT helped me break the Emotional Attachment

REBT helped me identify the irrational beliefs, like:

- "I need validation from others for finding a successful trade, especially when the trade is going against me."
- "People who are on social media platforms are better traders than me, and considering their viewpoint will make me a better trader."

Please understand I have really tried to analyze myself to the core, taking each aspect thread by thread. These things look very easy while reading, but when it comes to identifying the deeper emotions within ourselves, it becomes really hard.

Through REBT techniques, I challenged these beliefs:

Irrational Belief	Rational Replacement
"I need validation from other traders and experts."	"I only need to follow my strategy to the end. What others think of the market should not influence my trades."
"People who are on social media platforms are better traders, and considering their viewpoint will make me a better trader."	"I need to scan social media for any news that is against my current positioning, as my first job is to reduce risk. Searching for news and views in favor of my position will only increase my Confirmation Bias."

By stopping to give unnecessary importance to others' views on my trading outcomes, I became free to evaluate trades more objectively.

6.6 Reflection Exercise: Catch Your Confirmation Bias

Reflect on your last 5 to 10 trades. Be honest in your answers.

- After entering the trade, did you only seek supporting evidence?
- Did you feel happy and satisfied when you saw many experts in social media had similar views?
- Did you ignore warning signs that contradicted your view?
- Were you emotionally attached to being right?
- How could you have objectively evaluated counter–evidence?
- What rational belief can you apply to prevent this next time?

Build a habit of asking yourself: "What is the strongest argument against my current position?" Train your mind to do the uncomfortable task of seeking news, technical reports, which are against your position.

The market doesn't reward the most confident trader. It rewards the most objective one.

CHAPTER 7

ANCHORING BIAS: THE DANGER OF GETTING STUCK

> *"The phenomenon we were studying is so common and important in the everyday world that you should know its name: an anchoring effect."*
>
> – Daniel Kahneman

7.1 What is Anchoring Bias?

Anchoring bias is the tendency to **rely too heavily on the first piece of information we receive**, even if it becomes irrelevant later.

In trading, the anchor or the price at which we get fixed is often:

- Your entry price,
- The target you imagined,
- Or a price you have seen on a social media post or news article.

Once that anchor gets embedded, your mind keeps referencing it, even when the market conditions have changed.

Anchoring causes traders and investors to make poor decisions because they compare everything to the anchor, not to the present market reality.

7.2 How Anchoring Bias Shows Up in Trading

Situation	Anchor	Emotional Trap
You bought a stock at Rs 500.	Rs 500 becomes the anchor.	"The trend turns down, but you wait till it comes back to Rs 500."
Your target was Rs 700.	Market stalls at Rs 660 and turn lower.	"You wait as your mind is anchored at Rs 700."
You invest in a stock at Rs 100.	You exit at Rs 200 with a 100% profit. But the stock is still very strong and is moving up.	"You are not able to re-enter again as your mind is anchored at Rs 100, which was your initial buy. It is not letting you buy at a higher number again."
You read a report or watch a TV discussion suggesting the Nifty Index is headed to 30000.	That number sticks with your mind and becomes the anchor.	You hold on to long positions too long, ignoring the reversal signals.

Instead of adapting to what the chart is telling you now, your brain is stuck on what you fed it earlier. And in the ever volatile markets it is deadly.

7.3 My Struggles with Anchoring Bias

I have fallen into the trap of anchoring multiple times.

One particular example which comes to mind is my initial investment in a famous food delivery stock at the Rs 58 to Rs 60 region, watching for basing signs. The stock slowly moved to the Rs 100–120 region in the next 10 months, and I exited in that region.

The stock was still showing great strength, and it went on to make a time high of Rs 306. In between price had retraced at least 8 times to its 20d and 50d moving averages, giving good buy setups.

But then I couldn't buy as my anchor was fixed at Rs 58 – 60. I kept on waiting for similar levels to come to buy, which never happened.

I have learned this the hard way: "Price anchors are mental handcuffs. They stop you from acting on reality and trap you in fantasy."

7.4 How CBT helped me Unhook from Anchors

CBT taught me to notice why my decisions were based on **hope for a number.** Instead of logic from the chart of analysis.

My internal dialogue would sound like: "Let me wait a bit more – I will buy at my initial buy levels." I started challenging that thought with the help of CBT principles.

CBT Prompt	My Answer
"Is Rs 58 a magical number?"	No, it was just another entry. The market has no obligation towards me to come back to those levels.
"What is the chart telling me now?"	The market is still in an uptrend with key moving averages acting as strong supports.
"Is not entering again at supports on a strong uptrend, helping or hurting my long-term edge?"	It's hurting, and I am now reacting emotionally, not rationally.

CBT helped me to see the anchor and then actively question its validity.

7.5 How REBT helped me break the Emotional Fixation

REBT helped me go deeper by addressing the emotional demands behind fixating on the anchors.

I realized I often held irrational beliefs like:

- "I should be able to buy at the lowest possible price to tell my friends and colleagues that I am a successful investor or trader."
- "If I have a final target in mind, then it's the responsibility of market to hit it."
- "If a famous person has given a level in TV or on social media, then the price will surely reach there."

These beliefs made it emotionally painful to close trades early, enter into new trades even when logic demanded it. REBT taught me to dispute these beliefs.

Irrational Belief	Rational Replacement
"I should be able to buy at the lowest possible price to tell my friends and colleagues that I am a successful investor or trader."	It is not necessary to buy at the lowest price or sell at the highest price to be successful. My trading and investment profits are my responsibility, and other than the false emotional satisfaction, I don't get any value addition discussing my positions and profitability with my friends.

"If I have finalized a target in mind, then its markets responsibility to hit it."	The market has no responsibility towards me or my target levels. On a daily basis, I have to analyze charts and data flow rationally for any developments that could increase risk on my positions.
"If a famous person has given a level in TV or social media, then the price will surely reach there."	The person has given his or her view as per the data available at that point in time. Things change in the market in a second, and they might change their view too. Also, there is always a possibility of their view going wrong. So, I should not fixate on any levels given by others.

Once I stopped making price targets into emotional demands, I became more flexible and made fewer mistakes, which made my trading and investing more profitable.

7.6 Reflection Exercise: Let Go of the Anchor

Think of your trades where you feel you would have shown Anchor Bias:

- What was the entry price or target anchor?
- Did you stay emotionally attached to it?
- Did you ignore signs that invalidated the setup?
- What would a more rational, adaptive decision would have looked like?
- What new belief can you adopt to prevent anchoring next time?

Don't fight the market to prove your anchor was "right." Adjust it to protect your capital.

CHAPTER

8

RECENCY BIAS – TRAPPED IN THE LAST TRADE

"Your investment choices are distorted through the voice of your experience, and the louder the narrative, the more recent or dramatic, the greater the influence it has over your independent judgement."

– Coreen T Sol

8.1 What is Recency Bias?

Recency Bias is the tendency to place too much weight on recent experiences when making decisions, while ignoring the bigger picture or long-term probabilities.

In trading, Recency Bias often makes you believe that:

- The last trade outcome predicts what will happen next.
- The last few candles, days, or weeks define the whole trend.
- A few recent wins = You are invincible.
- A few recent losses = You are doomed.

Recency Bias distorts reality by making us emotionally attached to recent trades and thereby reducing the rational thinking process.

8.2 How Recency Bias Hurts Traders

Here is how it looks in action:

Recent Experience	Bias–Driven Behavior
3 or more losses in a row (3 is not a magic number. It can be 3 or 4 or any number of trades to affect you emotionally.)	You hesitate to take the next valid setup, fearing another loss.
3 or more wins in a row	You increase the position size recklessly, believing you are in the zone.
The last 2 breakout setups failed	You avoid the third one, even if it satisfies all your conditions.

Recency Bias makes you trade your past and not your present, and that kills consistency.

8.3 My Struggles with Recency Bias

Recency bias affected me in both winning and losing streaks, making me move towards the zone of Overconfidence or Loss Aversion.

After 3 to 4 winning trades, I would start believing I had cracked it. I would feel in the zone and get the rhythm of the market, or like my boss in the previous firm used to say, "You have started to catch the thread again". I should have taken it as a warning. Human beings like being congratulated and hearing good things about themselves. The confidence then slowly starts turning into carelessness. Many times, I would be so casual as to look only at the last candle and then take positions.

After 3 to 4 losing trades, the opposite happened. I would hesitate and doubt my setup. Even if the charts show clear pattern breakouts, I would freeze.

One specific week I remember when equity markets were in an uptrend and the majority of stocks were going up or consolidating. A lot of pattern breakouts were to be seen daily. I took a couple of triangle breakouts and went long, only to get stopped out as the price reversed quickly. After a few more failed breakouts, I started getting nervous about taking a trade again. The market was overall in consolidation, and hence, stocks were also taking more time to go higher.

Another setup came, and I was too afraid to take it. The Recency Bias in my mind screamed, "Don't take it. This one will also fail. Save yourself the pain."

I skipped the trade, and the setup worked this time, and this trade could have recovered everything and more. Many such failed trades made me realize that "a biased memory is not a trading system."

8.4 How CBT helped me regain perspective

CBT helped me recognize and remove the emotional loops caused by recent experiences.

I started recognizing the automatic thought patterns that Recency Bias created:

- "I am in a losing phase."
- "The last few trades failed, and this one probably will too."
- "The last few trades were a huge success. This is the time to hit it big."

Using CBT, I asked myself:

CBT Prompt	My Mental Response
"Am I judging the setup or my emotions from the last trade?"	"It is my emotion and I am stuck with it." The setup is valid and fulfills all criteria.
"Is this trade the same as the previous ones?"	No, it's a new chart, new structure, and even if the setup has come in the same asset, the market conditions could have changed. I have to analyze rationally.
After a losing streak, ask yourself this. "What would I do if this were my first trade of the week?"	I would take it without hesitation as it fulfills all criteria.

This mental separation between past trades and current setups became a game-changer.

8.5 How REBT helped me avoid attachment to the past

REBT helped me understand that Recency bias is not just about memory, it's an emotional baggage.

I discovered I had irrational beliefs like:

- "I need to avoid the pain of taking losses."
- "I need to make the maximum profit by taking risks more than normal when I am on a winning streak, else all my profits will be wiped away."
- "Taking huge risks which could seriously dent my account is acceptable when I am on a winning streak."

REBT helped me dispute and replace these beliefs:

Irrational Belief	Rational Replacement
"I need to avoid the pain of taking losses."	"I prefer not to lose, but every trade carries its own risk, and I can only manage the risk."
"I need to make the maximum profit by taking risks than normal when I am on a winning streak, else all my profits will be wiped away."	"This trade is one of many, and the next could be a winner or a loser. I should not risk losing everything on a single trade."
"Taking huge risks which could seriously dent my account is acceptable when I am on a winning streak."	"Again, the next trade has a good probability of becoming a loser. I should not risk more than what was decided in my strategy. Also, the past outcomes do not guarantee the next one will also be a successful trade."

Letting go of emotional residue from previous trades made me more centered and consistent, especially during tough weeks.

8.6 Reflection Exercise: Are you Trading your past?

Think about your recent ten trades:

- How did your recent trades influence your confidence or fear?
- Did you hesitate or overtrade because of recent outcomes?
- Did you treat a current trade objectively or did emotions take over you?
- What rational belief can you apply to treat each trade as a fresh one?

Before every trade, ask yourselves, If I had not taken any trades this week, would I still take this one right now?

If the answer is "Yes," then act.

If the answer is emotional, then pause.

The best traders don't carry their past into their next trade. They carry their processes.

CHAPTER 9

THE GAMBLER'S FALLACY – DUE FOR A WIN? OR DUE FOR A MISTAKE?

> "A gambler is nothing but a man who makes his living out of false hope."
>
> – William Bolitho

9.1 What is the Gamblers fallacy?

The Gambler's Fallacy is the belief that past outcomes affect future probabilities, especially in situations that are independent and random.

In trading, it shows up as:

- "I have had 5 losses in a row, the next one has to be a win."
- "This setup has failed me twice; the third time will work for sure."
- "I have lost money in the last few months, I am due for a big winner now."

This creates a false sense of certainty and leads to dangerous decisions like

- Start forcing trades,
- Taking bigger risks,

- Abandoning plans based on emotions and not your edge.

9.2 How the Gambler's Fallacy Hurts Traders

Here is how it typically looks

Situation	Gamblers Fallacy Response
3 trades in a row stopped out	You double the risk on the next trade, thinking, "It's due to work now."
5 green candles in the chart	You go short thinking, "A red candle has to come now."
Stock falls continuously for a few weeks	You start to think, "It has fallen a lot; how much more can it fall? It's time to buy it."
A strategy has not performed well for a while	You blindly take the next signal without the full setup getting triggered.

Please understand this is different from mean reversion trades. Mean reversion trades measure the extremity of movement to one side and then take a calculated risk on the opposite side. In the above examples, there is no strategy; it is just our expectation of the balance of things, not the market's current structure.

9.3 My Struggles with the Gambler's Fallacy

I have lived this bias in my early trading career and of course painfully.

Consider this scenario. You had a bullish view on the Equity Index. You start buying At the Money Index Call Option. Price falls to the next support and you buy more by averaging the same option (worse strategy) or buy more At the Money Call Options. Price falls again to next support, and you feel this is it. Price has fallen a lot and it is due to rally now. You add more of Call options.

The voice in your head says "You have done your part and taken a good position, market is due to rally now. Focus on what you will do with all the profits."

I have slowly taken a huge risk by increasing my position size, all the while telling myself it was logical. But it is not logic, and it was driven by a belief in fairness. The belief that price action will soon be fair to me is illogical.

The trade failed and the larger loss wiped out a years' worth of gains.

An important thing to note here is that these kind of losses significantly erode your confidence and will power for weeks or months.

I can remember many instances when I have asked this question to myself, "Why am I forcing my feelings on a market that doesn't care about my pain or my past?"

9.4 How CBT helped me break the Pattern

CBT helped me catch the distorted thoughts and behavior patterns behind the Gambler's Fallacy.

- "If I followed my plan and keep on taking positions with increased position size in that direction, the next trade will compensate for everything."
- "I plan to increase position size on each subsequent trade, and doing that will somehow save me and make my equity curve into profit."

With CBT, I started asking:

CBT Prompt	My Realization
"Is assuming the next trade will compensate the right thought?"	No, each trade is independent. The market doesn't care for my previous outcomes.
"Am I making emotional predictions?"	Yes, I am expecting balance when none is present.
"Am I looking at the risk I am taking in the account?"	No, I am blinded by emotions, and my risk management has gone for a toss.

This stopped me from escalating risk just because of frustration.

9.5 How REBT helped me reframe my Expectations

REBT helped me uncover the emotional demands beneath the behavior:

"I must be in profit now, or I am a loser."

"If I am not profitable every year, I cannot be successful."

These were irrational beliefs that created urgency and disappointment. Using REBT, I began to dispute these beliefs.

Irrational Belief	Rational Response
"The next trade must work for me to feel successful."	"No trade must do anything. My job is to take good trades, and my sanity is not linked to the trading outcome."

"I must be in profit now, or I am a loser."	"Again, the immediate trading outcome has no effect on who I am, provided I am following my trading plan."
"If I am not profitable every year, then I am not successful."	This belief actually forces me to take unnecessary risks, especially during year-end if I had bad months earlier. "My objective is to take the next best trade with proper risk management. If I am doing that consistently, then I have a good probability of being profitable at the end of the year."

This helped me emotionally detach from the expectation of a winning trade being due.

Now, when I face a losing streak, I remind myself – **"I don't need this trade to win – I just need to execute the next edge with discipline."**

9.6 Reflection Exercise: Are You Chasing a Win?

Think about your recent trading week.

- Have you ever increased position size after a losing streak?
- Did you ever think, "This one has to work?"
- Did you skip your process because of impatience or urgency?
- What would a rational, process-driven trader do in that moment?
- What new belief can help you avoid emotional chasing?

After few losses in a row don't let your risk management loose, tighten them as that's when the Gamblers Fallacy creeps in.

CHAPTER 10

THE ENDOWMENT EFFECT – FALLING IN LOVE WITH YOUR TRADES

"The heart has its reasons which reason does not know."

– Blaise Pascal

10.1 What is the Endowment Effect?

The Endowment effect is a psychological bias where we place a higher value on things we own, simply because we own them.

In trading, it looks like:

- You are giving emotional importance to your stock, your option, your trade more than the market, data, or your trading strategy giving it.
- You might think "This stock will go up, I have held it for more than a year. "It's my best performing stock, it deserves another chance.", "I have spent too much time in this trade to exit it now."

You become emotionally attached to the position. You stop looking at it with objectivity. And worst of all, you may refuse to exit even when data is screaming at you to do so.

10.2 How the Endowment Effect Traps Traders

Here is how it typically shows up:

Situation	Endowment Effect Response
Holding on to a losing trade or investment	"I cannot exit now. I have already invested so much time and money."
You have researched a stock deeply	"I know this stock and I believe in it. I am not like other traders, and I cannot go wrong."
You found a stock that is doing good till so far. You tell your friends and followers about it. You are now attached to your opinion through others, too.	"I have told everyone about this stock, but I shouldn't be selling it from my portfolio. I will look like a fool if the stock becomes a multi-bagger and I don't hold it.", "Or it is my responsibility towards them that this stock should work."

The more effort, time, research, or identity you associate with a trade, the harder it becomes to let go.

You fall in love with the trade or investment and stop seeing the chart and start seeing hope.

10.3 My Struggles with the Endowment Effect

I have gone through this mistake several times, but one experience stands out.

A few years back, I had invested in a stock that had good potential in the EV ecosystem. I had done good research, built conviction, and sized the position larger than usual. Initially, it moved in my direction, but later on, it started going below my comfort level. This happened after few months, and by that time it had become "My stock". I had told about it to my friends and family.

I held on because I was emotionally attached, and I had to be the guardian of that stock. My research on the stock had come to a literal zero. It was just hope and emotional attachment that was carrying the investment.

My mind kept on telling me:

- "I have researched this one too much – I can't be wrong."
- "I have held it for months; it might soon pay off."
- "I have held it for so long, and I have told everyone about it. If I exit and then the stock rallies, I will look like a fool."

Look how all these thought patterns take you away from protecting against risk. I kept checking the stock daily, even looking at minute charts for basing patterns, but refused to cut it.

Everyone has a pain threshold, and we do our irrational behavior till our mind and body can take it. Eventually, I exited. Not on my terms, but out of pain with a loss.

Markets don't pay you for being blindly loyal. It pays you for being rationally loyal to a trade or investment.

10.4 How CBT helped me see the Attachment

CBT helped me notice the thought traps I was falling into

- "I believed the stock was special because I had spent energy on it."
- "I believed exiting would mean all my research was wasted."
- "I felt betrayed when the trade didn't behave how I expected."
- "I felt responsible to be part of the trade as I had told everyone about it."

Using CBT, I began asking:

CBT Prompt	Mental Check
"Would I buy this trade if I hadn't already owned it?"	Most of the time the answer would be "NO".
"Am I holding this trade because of data or because of past attachment?"	It was usually the attachment.
"What emotion is driving this position?"	Hope. Not discipline.

This helped me separate what the trade was from what I felt about it.

10.5 How REBT helped me break Emotional Ownership

REBT helped me question the deeper irrational beliefs that made the endowment effect so sticky. Beliefs like:

- "If I exit now, all my research goes to waste."
- "Market rewards loyalty."
- "I have put too much effort into this. My credibility is attached to this. I should stick till it works."

Using REBT, I reframed these beliefs:

Irrational Belief	Rational Response
"If I exit now, all my research goes to waste."	"Effort doesn't guarantee outcome. Letting go is sometimes the smart move, especially when the market is not favoring the trade."

"Market rewards loyalty."	"The market doesn't reward blind loyalty and owes me nothing. My job is to manage risk and not hold hope."
"My credibility is attached to this trade or investment."	"Your credibility is not attached to a single trade, and exiting a bad trade early is a sign of maturity, not failure. "

The more I practiced this, the easier it became to look at positions with detachment. Detachment does not mean not participating in the market; it means keeping a healthy distance and watching over.

When I was young and played national level chess, my coach used to ask me to go and watch the board from a distance. I used to do this when things got complicated. This gives you a broader perspective of what was happening. This doesn't mean that I was not analyzing my moves or that I stopped watching the board. Similarly, watching markets from a different angle without many trades can give you an "Aha" moment. You will ask yourself, "How did I miss this earlier?"

I ask one question to you: "Would you still take this trade with all the knowledge you have as of today?" If the answer is No, then please exit. Don't hope.

10.6 Reflection Exercise: Are you Emotionally Invested?

Think about your current Open Positions (Trading & Investing)

- Which trades feel special or personal? Why?
- Are you holding anything just because you spend time/money on it?
- Have you ignored exit signals in a trade you feel attached to?
- What would a detached, rational decision look like?
- What belief is stopping you from exiting and what would be a better belief?
- What position would I not take today even though I still am holding it? Why am I still holding it?

Great traders don't fall in love with trades. They fall in love with discipline.

CHAPTER 11

THE QUIET BIASES THAT KEEP YOU STUCK – SUNK COST FALLACY & HERD MENTALITY

11.1 You already know these biases – But now it's time to Own Them

By now, you have walked through the heavy hitters:

- Loss Aversion
- Overconfidence
- Confirmation Bias
- Anchoring
- Recency
- Gamblers Fallacy
- Endowment Effect

These are loud, emotional, and destructive mental sirens.

But there are two more of them that don't scream. They just quietly convince you to **stay stuck, to not move, to follow or to freeze.**

11.2 Sunk Cost Fallacy – "I have come too far to Quit Now."

You have already lost 30% of your capital in an investment. You have held it for 2 years. You have added on dips.

And now you can't let it go – not because of what is coming, but because of what is already gone. That's the Sunk cost fallacy. You might be wondering. Isn't it similar to the Endowment effect? There is a slight difference.

The sunk cost fallacy happens when someone continues to invest time, money, or effort into something that is no longer rational because of prior investment. In contrast, endowment bias is the tendency to overvalue an item just because you own it.

Sunk Cost fallacy convinces you that exiting now is "wasting everything" and holding is "giving it one last chance."

But here is what I learned the hard way: "You don't recover losses by holding them, you recover by letting go of the need to be right."

11.3 Herd Mentality – "If Everyone's doing it, it must be right"

You will relate to this one.

You log in to social media and see someone talking about a breakout in a particular stock. You search for the name of that stock and see many others suggesting the same on Twitter. You go to Telegram and see the stock's name being discussed there, suggesting "BUY". There are many videos on YouTube suggesting the same.

Minutes ago you didn't know about the stock, but now you are all in.

That's Herd Mentality, the emotional safety of the crowd. It feels easier to be wrong with everyone than to be right alone.

It feels smarter to agree than to pause and ask, "Does this align with my system?"

But I have learned "When you outsource your system and conviction, you lose control of the results."

11.4 Time to Step Up: Use what you have learned

By now, you have seen the patterns. You have practiced CBT tools and REBT frameworks.

This chapter won't guide you step by step again. Because now it's your turn to build awareness and discipline on your own.

Reflection and Reset: Spotting Your Quiet Biases

Sunk Cost Fallacy

- What position are you still holding, mainly because you have already lost too much?
- What emotions come up when you think about exiting that trade?
- What irrational beliefs are keeping you there? (Use CBT/REBT models to work through it)
- What would a neutral, data-driven decision look like?
- Write this sentence:
"Even though I have lost _____, I choose to _____ because it protects my future decisions."

Herd Mentality

- Recall 2 to 3 trades you entered mainly because someone else was bullish or bearish.
- What were your thoughts before entering? What was your emotion?
- How often do you follow the crowd even when your system says something else?
- What belief could help you trade with more inner conviction? (Try a CBT-style reframing)

- Complete this sentence:
"I trust my method more than the market noise because _____."

These two – Sunk Cost fallacy and Herd mentality may not shout like the others, but they are no less dangerous.

They don't attack your logic, but they exploit your fear, your pride, and your need to belong.

You now have the tools:

- CBT to catch the automatic thoughts.
- REBT to challenge your irrational beliefs.
- Reflection to pause and realign.

What you do with those tools is entirely yours. The next section will take us into a deeper space – the emotional distortions that don't just affect your trading, but they affect how you see yourself.

But before we go there, pause, reflect, and own your mind. Because Biases don't just disappear. They just wait for the next unprepared moment.

SECTION 4
MASTERING COGNITIVE DISTORTIONS

CHAPTER 12

TRANSITIONING FROM TRAPS TO TRUTH – MOVING INWARD

> *"Man is the only kind of varmint who sets his trap, baits it, and then steps in it."*
>
> **– John Steinbeck**

You have just walked through some of the most invisible and dangerous traps that exist in trading:

- You have seen how the mind anchors to numbers that no longer matter.
- You have seen how overconfidence feels like clarity, right before a fall.
- You have seen how loss aversion, sunk costs, and the crowd can pull you away from your system and into chaos.

These are cognitive biases and are errors in judgment. They distort how we see the market.

But there is another layer beneath that. The deeper layer and the one most traders never look at.

It's not about how you perceive the market; it's about how you view yourself – whether you win, lose, feel uncertain, or are just exhausted.

This is the world of cognitive distortions.

12.1 From Behavior to Belief

Biases make you act against your plan. But distortions?

- They make you doubt yourself.
- They make you judge yourself.
- They make you feel like your performance is your personality.

I have discussed this feeling with my trader friends. "Why does one losing week feel like my entire identity just collapsed?" Initially, I tried to find answers in charts and reports.

But later, I understood that the answer is in the "**story I was telling myself about the chart.**"

I was able to separate my negative thoughts, like:

- "I will never recover."
- "I am not cut out for this."
- "Why does this always happen to me?"

These aren't tactical errors. They are emotional distortions and are invisible narratives that hijack your clarity and crush your confidence.

12.2 What you will Learn Next

In the next section, we will look at:

- The thoughts that spiral after a single bad trade or a few trades.
- The emotional beliefs that turn discomfort into defeat.
- The irrational patterns that traders repeat without ever realizing it.

You will see how your brain reacts when fear spikes, when control slips, and when shame creeps in.

And most importantly, you will learn to catch those reactions, challenge them, and change them.

This is not the easy part of the book. This is the honest part.

If you have ever:

- Overreacted to one loss.
- Quit a good trading system because of emotion.
- Thought you were not good enough for this game.
- Or felt like you were on a mental roller coaster through the week.

Then what's coming next might be the most important part of this book for you.

Let's go inward now. Let's rebuild the part of the system that no one else can define and do for you, and only you can. Let's rebuild your mind.

CHAPTER 13

THE INVISIBLE NARRATOR – UNDERSTANDING COGNITIVE DISTORTIONS IN TRADING

"Trading is very competitive and you have to be able to handle getting your butt kicked."

– Paul Tudor Jones

13.1 What are Cognitive Distortions?

Cognitive distortions, identified by Dr. Aaron Beck, are irrational thought patterns that skew our perception of reality, especially in emotional situations. They are exaggerated form of cognitive biases that can lead to negative emotions and dysfunctional behaviors.

They are mental habits we fall into when under stress, like:

- Jumping to conclusions
- Overgeneralizing
- Catastrophizing
- Thinking in extremes
- Taking everything personally

They are not flaws. They are not signs of weakness. They are mental filters or short shortcuts, or patterns that our brain has practiced for years to protect us from fear, shame, or disappointment.

But in trading, these distortions become traps.

Because when you distort reality, you can no longer trust your thinking. And if you can't trust your mind, then how do you trust your next trade?

13.2 Why Cognitive Distortions Matter to Traders

As traders, you are constantly exposed to:

- Uncertainty
- Volatility
- Emotional highs and lows
- Risk of financial and psychological loss

Cognitive distortions don't just influence your emotions, but they also dictate your actions:

- Exiting too early
- Holding too long
- Avoiding trades
- Overtrading
- Giving up after a losing streak
- Risking everything to "prove something"

And the worst part – you usually don't even know you are distorting.

13.3 The Most Common Cognitive Distortions in Trading

Here are the key ones we will explore, along with how they typically show up:

1. **Catastrophizing** – "One loss means everything is falling apart." You exaggerate the impact of a loss or event and spiral into panic, hopelessness, or shutdown.
2. **All or Nothing Thinking** – "I am a failure if I am not winning." You view outcomes in extremes – perfect or disaster, success or failure, with no middle ground.
3. **Emotional Reasoning** – "I feel anxious, so this trade must be wrong." You treat your emotions as facts. If you feel fear, you believe something is wrong, even when it's not.
4. **Overgeneralization** – "Last time this happened, I lost. So, I will lose again." You draw general conclusions based on one or two events, and turn isolated outcomes into universal rules.
5. **Labeling** – "I am such a loser." You define your identity based on one or a few trading outcomes – turning a moment into a verdict on who you are.

13.4 What Cognitive Distortions Feel Like

Distortions don't sound like psychology in your head. They sound like self-talk:

- "I can't take another loss."
- "I am not good at this."
- "This always happens to me."
- "I knew I would be wrong again."
- "I should have known it better."
- "Everyone else is successful – Why am I not?"

They feel real because you have practiced them for years. But they are not the truth. They are the untrained mental habits under pressure.

13.5 How we will work with them

In the next few chapters, we will go deeper into the 5 most common distortions seen in traders.

For each, you will learn:

- What is the cognitive distortion?
- How it shows up in trades.
- How does it feel inside you
- How I have personally struggled with it.
- How CBT and REBT helped me shift.
- Reflection tools to catch and challenge them.

This is not about fixing yourself. You are not broken. You are just believing thoughts that don't serve you.

This section will shed light on the thinking patterns that you have never questioned. And once you see the pattern, you get the power to rewrite it.

CHAPTER 14

CATASTROPHIZING – WHEN ONE LOSS FEELS LIKE THE END

> *"It was just a loss on the chart. But in my head, it became the end of everything."*
>
> – Anonymous

14.1 Emotional Trigger

I was extremely worried. I was not sure whether there was any point in this life. I was not able to talk to family, enjoy even a moment with them. I was just staring at the trades, not able to do anything. I had stopped out of a few of them, feeling extreme pain.

I was not able to look at P&L numbers, and when I looked at them, I was not looking at the numbers. I was staring at my fears.

You would have felt this emotion at least once in your trading career. You feel it building, and negative and irrational thoughts take over:

- "This is it. I have ruined everything."
- "What if I never recover?"
- "What if I was never meant for this?"
- "Why did I leave my job?"

- "Where is God? Can't he or she see my pain?"

You don't just lose the trade. You lose your confidence, your momentum, and your sense of control.

This is Catastrophizing – the mental distortion where one bad moment is blown into a life-defining disaster.

14.2 What is Catastrophizing?

Catastrophizing is a cognitive distortion where your brain exaggerates problems, assuming the worst possible outcome. It makes you react as if the worst-case scenario is already happening.

In trading, it sounds like:

- "If I lose again, I am finished."
- "None of my systems are working. Maybe nothing ever will."
- "I will never improve in trading."
- "I can never be a profitable trader."

The list can go on, and it will be unique for each one of you. It's not about what is real. It's about what you believe is about to happen, and that belief ruins your mind.

14.3 The Spiral in Trading

Here's how it plays out

A small loss- Emotional discomfort- Imagined disaster ------- Identity collapse

The danger isn't the trade itself. It's the meaning you give it. You are no longer thinking about a 2% to 4% drawdown. You are thinking about:

- Your career
- Your worth

- Your future
- Your deepest fears

And that is the trap. **A moment becomes a meltdown.**

14.4 My Experience: When One Trade Became Everything

There was a month in my trading journey when I faced severe losses. I paused my trading for some time and started small again. Things started working well for some time, and my confidence was back. Suddenly, there was a week again when I faced four losses in a row.

All within plan, small, and my risk parameters. Then came the fifth trade. I was getting anxious already, and it also failed.

To an outside observer, this would seem like a normal situation; everyone knows that a losing streak can happen occasionally. However, inside me, something shattered.

My mind started thinking uncontrollably:

- "I have given everything to this."
- "Why am I still failing after all these years?"
- "What if I never become successful?"
- "How will I face my ex-colleagues if I am a loser in trading?"

I was not crying for money; I was stunned to see my belief in getting better at trading shattered.

That's the weight of Catastrophizing. It turns effort into regret, a trade into threat, and the trading itself into a useless exercise. You start to project the worst-case scenario into everything.

I skipped setups for days. I stopped trusting myself. The discipline was lacking, and journaling stopped.

I want to discuss this part a bit more. **Every time I had such instances, the first thing to get destroyed was my discipline, and journaling was the first thing to stop. My mind made me think like "What is the use of all this?", "Why do I have to revisit all the losing trades and go through the pain again when I can avoid it?".**

It wasn't the trade that broke me. It was the story I built around it.

14.5 What CBT taught me

CBT helped me slow down, pause, and reflect.

I started asking:

Automatic Thought	CBT Reframe
"This means I am a failure."	"What does the data say? Have I followed my process?"
"It is over."	"Is this the end? Or just a difficult period?"
"I can't bounce back from this."	"I have bounced back before too, and this time will not be different."

CBT didn't erase my pain immediately, but it helped me view the pain and the pain-creating scenario rationally.

It helped me stop telling myself: "This is everything," and instead say: "This is just one thing."

14.6 How REBT helped me think differently

Catastrophizing is not just random thoughts. They are emotional reactions to the irrational beliefs you carry. With REBT, I realized I was holding on to several of them, like:

- "I must succeed quickly, or it means I am not good enough."
- "This should not be happening to me."
- "I can't handle another loss."

These "musts" and "shoulds" created unnecessary pressure and broke me when reality didn't obey them. Using REBT, I rewrote these demands:

Irrational Belief	Rational Response
"I must always win."	"Losing is not failure. Markets are volatile, and you had anticipated this happening sometimes."
"This should not be happening to me."	"I am not special for the market to treat me like one. This moment is unpleasant, but I can respond properly. Both emotionally and execution wise."
"I can't go through this again."	"I have gone through this phase many times. I continue to learn and try my best not to repeat mistakes. I will go through it again."

I don't need every trade to work. I need to work on how I react to each trade.

14.7 Reflection: Defusing the Disaster Story

Write freely, honestly. No filters.

- What was the last trade or moment that made you feel like everything was falling apart?
- What were the first automatic thoughts that followed?
- What was the imagined worst case scenario you built in your head?
- What actually happened?
- What belief do you need to challenge to stop this distortion next time?

Complete this line: "Even though I feel _____, I know the truth is _____."

Repeat after me: "I am very confident that I can rebuild, one thought at a time."

CHAPTER 15

ALL OR NOTHING THINKING – "IF I AM NOT WINNING EVERYTHING, I AM A FAILURE."

"While perfectionism can show up in many small, private ways, it tends to present along similar lines of all-or-nothing thinking."

– Liz Fosslien

15.1 Emotional Trigger

I feel a strange kind of emptiness after some trades. I win, but it doesn't feel satisfying. Instead of celebrating the process and respecting discipline, your mind says:

- "This win is too small."
- "I should have made more."
- "If I were really good, I would have caught the bigger move."

You are not competing with yourself, but with an exaggerated, imaginary version of you that never misses, always catches the highs and lows, and never tires.

This is All or Nothing thinking wrapped inside perfectionism, where success doesn't feel successful. Where anything less than perfect feels like a failure.

Please note that all or nothing thinking can also be seen without perfectionism, an example would be in relationships. I am focusing on what I feel impacts more on traders as All or Nothing thinking is closely related to perfectionism and is more dangerous to traders.

15.2 What is All or Nothing Thinking?

All or Nothing thinking, also called Black and White thinking, is a cognitive distortion where:

- Outcomes are seen as either total success or total failure.
- Process is ignored until it's perfect.
- Small win, steady growth, survival - are all seen as "not enough."

In trading, it sounds like:

- "If I didn't catch the whole move, it wasn't a good trade."
- "If I didn't have a perfect month, I am a loser."
- "Small profits don't matter. Only the big ones count."

There is no middle ground. Things are seen as success so perfect that it barely exists else its constant failure.

15.3 My Experience: Perfectionism and Missing My Progress

There was a period when my trading was going very well. I was following my plan, entry only based on setups, disciplined exits, and proper risk management. On paper, it was my best trading performance.

But internally, I felt nothing, and every win was dismissed:

- "Could have held longer."
- "Could have sized bigger."
- "Could have taken the earlier breakout."

Instead of anchoring on what I was doing right, I was obsessing on the few percentages I missed.

A point to note here. There is something called Behavioral Conditioning in Psychology (Associated with Ivan Pavlov, John B Watson, and B.F. Skinner). If you are working in a trading firm and your boss or senior colleagues who control your trading have an issue with All or Nothing Thinking, or for that matter, any other cognitive distortion, it rubs off on you. You start to develop those traits, too. Please work on yourself to understand what all these distortions are how you can be strong against them.

With time:

- Small wins felt like failures.
- Steady growth felt slow.
- And any small slip felt like the confirmation that "I am not capable."

15.4 How CBT Helped Me See the Middle Ground

CBT helped me step back from the brutal mental measurement. I began asking myself:

Automatic Thought	CBT Reframe
"This win isn't big enough."	"Did I follow my plan? Did my targets hit? If yes, that counts more than the size."
"I am always missing opportunities."	"I can make consistent returns, and my equity curve is steadily going up. That matters more than catching the lows and highs."

| "It's not enough." | "Enough compared to what? Am I becoming more disciplined or chasing fantasy?" |

CBT helped me realize that growth doesn't have to happen in extremes and success is not always a life and death event.

Every good trade, even imperfect, builds the future I am aiming for.

15.5 How REBT helped me Challenge Unrealistic Demands

REBT took the healing even deeper.

I realized I was placing irrational demands on myself, like:

- "I must maximize every opportunity."
- "I must trade at the highest level always."
- "I am incompetent if I miss a trade."

Through REBT disputation, I started reframing these emotions.

Irrational Demand	Rational Response
"I must catch the entire move."	"I prefer catching bigger moves, but partial wins build steady equity and keep me mentally sane."
"I must be flawless."	"No trader is flawless. Real success comes from resilience, not perfection."
"Small wins don't matter."	"Small wins are the building blocks of financial freedom."

I keep reminding myself, "I allow myself to succeed imperfectly."

It sounds simple, but when you truly accept it, you stop draining energy into chasing illusions. You start respecting the real wins you are already creating.

15.6 Reflection: Healing the Need for Perfection

Think about your trading journey and be honest with yourself.

- When was the last time you were not happy of a win or progress?
- What unrealistic comparison or expectation were you using against yourself?
- How would you describe that event if you used a positive and growth mindset?
- What does success look like to you, if it includes discipline, patience and imperfection?
- Complete this: "Even when it's not perfect, my work is building _____."

CHAPTER 16

EMOTIONAL REASONING – WHEN FEELINGS PRETEND AS FACTS

> "Emotional reasoning is among the most common of all cognitive distortions; most people would be happier and more effective if they did less of it."
>
> – **Jonathan Haidt**

16.1 Emotional Trigger

You plan the trades, you run the data, you check the setup. Everything aligns.

Still, as you try to press the "Buy" or "Sell" button in the broker terminal, your stomach tightens.

- "Something is not right."
- "I don't know if I can trust this."
- "What if this trade blows up?"

The fear is not coming from the chart or data. It is coming from inside you. And in that moment, the emotion feels like evidence.

This is Emotional Reasoning – the distortion where your feelings are treated as proof for objective reality.

I have a strong connection with this cognitive distortion. As someone with depression and anxiety, I often misinterpret my feelings as reality. During periods of high anxiety, my mind convinces me that something bad is happening or will happen, despite lacking any evidence. It's just a feeling I experience in my mind and body.

Emotional Reasoning makes you think and believe:

- If you feel anxious, something must be wrong.
- If you feel uncertain, your plan must be flawed.
- If you feel fear, disaster is around the corner.

But emotions and feelings are not reality. They are signals not certainties.

16.2 What is Emotional Reasoning

Emotional Reasoning is a cognitive distortion where you:

- Judge situations based purely on emotional reactions.
- Mistake internal discomfort for external danger.
- Trust fear, doubt, or hesitation more than evidence or process.

In trading, it sounds like:

- "I feel scared, so I must be wrong about this trade."
- "I feel uneasy, so my system must be failing."
- "I am nervous about this, so it must be better to avoid this opportunity."

It is not that the trade is broken. IT is that emotional turbulence makes you distrust yourself and your preparation.

16.3 My Experience: Trusting Feelings Over Facts

I still remember my first losing phase after leaving my job. I had sold a lot of out-of-the-money covered calls and even out-of-money naked calls. My objective was to collect a premium which would make me feel emotionally good, equivalent to my previous salary. This was a disaster waiting to happen, and it happened. The market rallied, and I had taken positions well above my risk profile. Soon, I had to cut the positions at a loss.

Days went by and I again saw an opportunity to sell covered calls and maybe some far out-of-the-money naked Index calls as the market was showing signs of fatigue. I decided I'll go for this trade. But the next morning, as the market opened, I felt this surge of hesitation.

- "What if I am wrong again?"
- "Maybe market will hit my stop loss and go up again."
- "It doesn't feel right."

Many times, like in the above situation, I have skipped excellent trades, not because the market invalidated them. Not because my strategy changed.

Because I trusted a fleeting emotion more than a prepared plan. You can imagine what would have happened next.

When I skipped the trade and watched it work without me, I felt even worse. It was a cycle of self–sabotage built on emotions pretending to be facts.

16.4 How CBT Helped Me Separate Feelings from Evidence

CBT gave me a critical mindset shift: "Feelings are not verdicts. They are many time inaccurate and are often exaggerated."

I started preparing for simple emotional separation:

Emotional Thought	CBT Check
"I feel anxious about this setup."	"Is the setup broken, or am I just scared?"
"I feel doubtful about taking the position."	"Is the doubt based on data or past emotional baggage?"
"I feel overwhelmed."	"Am I seeing new risks or is it just old fears resurfacing?"

I was able to separate my feelings and emotions from reality. I still felt fear, but I stopped letting fear mean something automatically without evidence.

16.5 How REBT Helped Me Dismantle Emotional Absolutes.

Through REBT, I was able to identify irrational beliefs underneath Emotional Reasoning.

Beliefs like:

- "I must feel certain before I act."
- "I must feel confident to be competent."
- "If I am feeling scared, I am making a mistake."

These demands made it difficult to execute trades. Most of the time, it was anxiety pretending to be logic.

Using REBT, I rewrote them

Irrational Belief	Rational Response
"I must feel certain before trading."	"Certainty is rare. The process is reliable. Feelings will come and go."
"If I am scared, the trade must be wrong."	"Fear is in human nature, and it can exist even when probabilities are in my favor."
"I need to be 100% confident before taking the trade."	"I need to only watch for my setup to trigger and use proper risk management to enter into a trade."

I started believing that it is OK to feel uncomfortable and still execute the plan.

16.6 Reflection: Feelings Not Equal to Fact

Take a few quiet minutes

- Recall a trade where emotion overruled your plan.
- What specific feeling triggered your hesitation or change?
- Was the trade plan invalid or was the emotion overwhelming?
- What would a calm, disciplined trader have done with the same information?
- Complete this: "Even when I feel_____, I choose to act based on _____."

CHAPTER 17

OVERGENERALIZATION – WHEN ONE LOSS BECOMES A LIFE PATTERN

> "Remember, the best traders think in a number of unique ways. They have acquired a mental structure that allows them to trade without fear and, at the same time, keeps them from becoming reckless and committing fear based errors."
>
> – Mark Douglas

17.1 Emotional Trigger

A few bad trades, one bad month. And suddenly your mind starts writing a bigger, darker story:

- "This always happens to me."
- "I can never catch a trend."
- "Every time I try something new, I fail."
- "I am not just lucky in the markets."

This is Overgeneralization – where a few painful experiences become permanent identity labels. Instead of seeing struggles as temporary, you start seeing them as a permanent part of your trading journey.

17.2 What is Overgeneralization?

Overgeneralization is a cognitive distortion where you:

Take one or two negative experiences and wrongly assume that they will happen again and again. You build a permanent negative story about yourself, your trading, and your future based on very limited evidence.

In trading, this sounds like:

- "Breakouts never work out for me."
- "Every time I follow a system, I fail."
- "Whenever I trade before or after the company announces results, I lose."

Instead of learning from experiences, you start to predict doom based on fear.

You stop seeing each trade as a new opportunity and start seeing it as a repeat of old pain.

17.3 Time for You to Step In

Instead of me sharing my personal story this time, I want you to catch your mind at work. Use the ABCDE framework we learned in chapter ….

Your Reflection Exercise: Catch and Reframe

1. A (Activating Event): What recent event triggered a negative story in your mind?
2. B (Belief): What generalization did you instantly jump to?
3. C (Consequence): How did that belief affect your emotions or actions?
4. D (Disputation): What specific evidence challenges that belief?
5. E (Effective New Belief): What more balanced, rational view can you adopt?

Be honest. And be compassionate to yourself. You are not here to judge yourself. You are here to free yourself.

CHAPTER

18

LABELING – WHEN ONE MISTAKE DEFINES WHO YOU ARE

> "One emotionally driven investment that causes massive losses is enough to keep you away from all investments for life."
>
> – **Naved Abdali**

18.1 Emotional Trigger

Mistakes happen. But instead of saying:

- "I made a mistake." You say, "I am a mistake."
- "That was a bad decision." You think: "I am a bad trader."

This is Labeling. This happens when you take an event or behavior and turn it into your whole identity.

18.2 What is Labeling?

Labeling is a cognitive distortion where:

- You define yourself entirely by a single event, mistake, or emotion.
- You use harsh, judgmental words against yourself.
- You turn behavior (what you did) into identity (who you are).

In trading, it sounds like:

- "I am a fool."
- "I am stupid for missing that move."
- "I am a failure because I lost again."

Instead of seeing mistakes as temporary, you wear them like your personality.

Labeling destroys confidence faster than any loss ever would. Because once you label yourself negatively, you stop trying to change and accept that you can't.

18.3 How Labeling Cripples Traders

Situation	Labeling Reaction
Bad entry timing	"I am clueless."
Exiting too early	"I am a coward."
Missing a big move	"I am hopeless."

Labeling destroys your self-trust. It creates emotional anchors that make you:

- Trade defensively out of fear.
- Quit too early.
- Stop evolving because you see yourself as flawed at the core

18.4 Now It's Your Turn to Work Through It

Using the ABCDE method again – this time for how you label yourself after trades or tough periods.

Your Reflection Exercise: Labeling and Identity Reset

1. A (Activating Event): What recent mistake triggered a harsh label in your mind?
2. B (Belief): What name or identity did you give yourself after it?
3. C (Consequence): How did that label affect your trading mindset or confidence?
4. D (Disputation): What facts show that this label is unfair or exaggerated?
5. E (Effective New Belief): What more compassionate, accurate description of yourself can you adopt?

Take your time. Speak to yourself the way you would speak to a good friend of yours.

CHAPTER 19

THE JOURNEY WE JUST TOOK

> "You do not trade the markets. You can only trade your beliefs about the markets."
>
> – Dr. Van K. Tharp

You have gone through some of the deepest emotional traps a trader faces:

- The spiral of Catastrophizing – when one loss feels like the end.
- The self-judgment of All or Nothing Thinking – when good isn't good enough.
- The self-doubt of Emotional Reasoning – when feelings pretend to be facts.
- The learned helplessness of Overgeneralization – when one mistake becomes a life sentence.
- The self-attack of Labeling – when you define yourself by your worst moments.

You might have found some chapters familiar, while others felt more painful. They could have shown you just how many games the mind plays under pressure and stress.

And that is what we want to achieve. To be able to see and detach from these distortions. **Now that you have seen it, you can fight it.**

19.1 Why This Work Matters More Than Any Strategy

Most traders think they need:

- Better Indicators
- Better setups
- Better market news flow

But what they need is:

- Better self – awareness
- Better emotional tolerance
- Better mental flexibility

You could have the perfect system in the world, but if you are catastrophizing after a small loss, or overgeneralizing a tough week into a permanent story, you will sabotage yourself no matter what the charts say.

Every bias you spot, every distortion you understand and fight, makes you regain power over your trading mind.

19.2 You Are Already Stronger Than When You Started

If you have read this far, if you have reflected, paused, and questioned, then you are already doing the work most traders will never do.

- You are seeing the traps before you step into them.
- You are questioning the stories you used to believe blindly.
- You are rewiring the mental foundation you trade from.

And when you change the mind you bring to the market, you change your trading outcomes too.

19.3 What's Next?

In the next section, we will build something even more practical:
- A Trader's Mental Toolbox – real exercises, real reframes, and real inner upgrades.
- Techniques you can use daily or weekly to stay strong when the market tests you.

Recognizing your biases and distortions is just the beginning. Now, it's time to train the mind that handles your money, your time, and your dreams.

Let's get to work.

SECTION 5
STRENGTHENING THE TRADER PSYCHE

CHAPTER 20

TRADER'S MENTAL TOOLBOX – BUILDING YOUR INNER EDGE

> *"Don't worry about what the markets are going to do, worry about what you are going to do in response to the markets."*
>
> **– Michael Carr**

20.1 Why You Need a Mental Toolbox

After walking through the traps of biases and distortions, you now know something most traders never realize:

- The biggest battles aren't outside you – they are inside
- The real enemy isn't market volatility – it's emotional volatility.
- It's not about avoiding fear, greed, or doubt – it's about having the tools to respond when they show up.

Now it's time to go beyond awareness. It is time to equip yourself. Trading is all about having the tools ready when cognitive biases and distortions inevitably arise.

You need tools that ground you, tools that bring you back to reality, tools that rebuild trust when your mind tries to tear you down.

When emotional storms hit – and they will – you will not be helpless like before. You will be equipped to handle them. This is what truly separates surviving traders from those who thrive.

20.2 The Tools I Wished I Had Sooner

I did not make my mental toolbox during the good phases. I built it after blowing my trades. After sabotaging winning systems. After convincing myself "I am not fit to be a world-class trader or investor" over and over again.

Every tool I share here is from my experience, and they have changed shapes and forms throughout the years. They are not theories to read and forget.

You will make it yours only if you follow them religiously. And I am very confident that the more you use it, you will change it, modify it to suit your psyche. And that's absolutely fine and is the right way. No one thing works for everyone. But start doing it and you will see results.

20.3 The Trader's Mental Toolbox

Here are the tools that helped me. They helped me in following a trading plan, following risk management and position sizing, sticking to the plan even when emotions were running high and low, and to survive those periods when everything seemed lost.

1. The Thought Catcher

The moment you notice a fearful thought, a dangerous prediction, or a perfectionistic demand – **Pause. Catch it. Label it.**

Ask yourselves:

- "Is it catastrophizing?"
- "Is it all-or-nothing thinking?"
- "Is it emotional reasoning?"

Before it becomes your belief, **name it**.

Naming the thought weakens the hold over you.

2. The Reality Anchor

When emotion overwhelms you, your first job is to return to objective reality.

Ask yourselves:

- What is the setup telling me?
- What is my system rule in this situation?
- What data am I ignoring because I am emotional?
- Is there any news or data that is against my position, adding to the risk?

Anchor back to facts, not fears.

3. The Belief Challenger

Use REBT techniques to challenge rigid emotional beliefs:

- "I must always win" – "No, although I like to win, I can survive losses too."
- "This should not happen to me." – "Market owes me nothing, reality is neutral to me. My losses and Gains are my responsibility."

Your strengths grow when your demands shrink.

4. The Emotional Reset Button

Simple tools to reset emotional chaos mid–trading. Do this at the start of your day, in the middle of the day, and after the trading session is over.

- Box breathing for 2 minutes. Developed by US Navy Seals to manage stress and improve performance, this helps you regain calm when things are going out of control. This technique involves breathing in, holding the breath, breathing out, and holding the breath. You can use 3-3-3-3 seconds for each step or 4-4-4-4 as per your convenience. Initially, it might feel a bit tough, but soon you will see your body and mind calm down.
- Writing a quick "thought-dump" on paper whenever you feel you need to do something other than your trading plan. Start observing your feelings when these thoughts come. Slowly, you will be able to see patterns in your thoughts, feelings, and behavior. When it happens, do box breathing and slow down yourself.
- Practice 3 calming self-affirmations ("I trust my process.", "I am capable.", "I can follow my trading plan"). You can choose any affirmations to your liking or check the **bonus affirmations page** of this book.

Reset your nervous system before and during the trading day.

5. The Confidence Builder

When self-doubt creeps in:

- List 3 tough trading situations you navigated successfully.
- Remind yourself: resilience and discipline define a trader. Results follow.

Your past struggles contain proof of your future strength.

6. The Discipline Dial

On emotional days, your job is not to be perfect – **It is to dial down risk and dial up process and discipline.**

- Reduce position sizing if you are mentally foggy – I am very confident that the majority of us would increase the position size here.
- Simplify steps if overwhelmed. Sometimes, take a break too. That is more difficult for many.

Adjust the "discipline dial" based on mental weather.

7. The Patience Timer

Use deliberate pauses before major trading actions:

- Before entering a trade.
- Before revenge trading after a loss.
- Before exiting too early out of fear.

Insert a space between emotion and action. Use box breathing as part of this space to calm your mind, along with reducing your impulsivity.

8. The Risk Radar

Before each session, ask:

- "How much am I risking emotionally and just not financially?"
- "Is this trade worth the mental energy it will consume?"

Your risk management is not just technical, it's psychological too. Because trades not only ruin you financially, it ruins you emotionally too.

9. The Focus Filter

Before each session:

- Define what information matters today.

- Block out everything else.
- Trust your filter, avoid FOMO.

Attention and will power are both finite and should be spent wisely.

10. The Gratitude Journal

At the end of the week:

- Write 3 things you did right, regardless of profits.
- Appreciate the lessons, discipline, and the showing up.
- Say thanks to the opportunity to be able to participate in one of the toughest professions in the world actively.

Gratitude is not just spiritual. It is psychological armor.

20.4 This Toolbox Will Not Make You Perfect

It will make you Resilient.

You will still feel fear sometimes. You will still hesitate sometimes. You will still lose trades. But you will stop losing yourself in the process.

These tools don't erase emotions. They help you navigate emotions with clarity and strength.

And slowly, trade by trade, day by day, you will build something far more valuable than profits:

- Your Self-trust.
- Your Emotional Toughness.
- Your Resilience.

20.5 How to Start Using These Tools

- Pick 2 to 3 tools to start practicing this week.
- Don't wait for a "perfect emotional storm" – practice even on good days.
- Track what tools work best for different emotional situations.
- Gradually integrate all 10 into your mental operating system over 90 days. Once you have completed reading the book, you can check the bonus section for a sample plan.

Because true trading mastery doesn't happen in your charts. It happens in your mind.

"In the end, your biggest trading asset is not a system. It's a mind that refuses to collapse under pressure."

Let's start building it – One tool at a time.

CHAPTER
21

TRADER'S BEHAVIORAL TOOLBOX – BUILD HABITS THAT HOLD

"The key to trading success is emotional discipline. if intelligence were the key, there would be a lot more people making money trading."

– Victor Sperandeo

21.1 Traders' Behavioral Toolbox

Simple tools to help you do the right thing, even when your emotions try to take over. You might already know what not to do – chase price, exit early, revenge trade. But how many times have you caught yourself doing it anyway?

That's the gap between knowing and doing. And the gap is where behavior lives.

This chapter is a small toolbox – five simple tools I personally use which can help you turn your mental awareness into real trading discipline. Use them the way you use your trading setup, regularly without searching for perfection.

1. The 5-Step Trade Entry Pause

Before any trade, give yourself 15-20 seconds to run through the list. Stick it on your wall, your screen, or journal. If you can't check them all, skip the trade.

- Am I trading my plan?
- Is this setup clean, or am I forcing it?
- Have I checked the broader context (Index trend, news)?
- Am I emotionally stable right now?
- Have I taken 3 slow breaths?

You will be shocked to see how many trades vanish with just these checks.

2. Daily Bias Reflection

Biases creep in when you are not looking. This short reflection helps you stay one step ahead. Every day after the market closes, ask yourself.

- What was the dominant mental bias today?
- Did it help or hurt me?
- What can I do to handle it better tomorrow?

Take 3 to 5 minutes to reflect on the above questions. It will push you ahead of 90% of traders.

3. Behavioral Scorecard

At the end of each week, give yourself a score between 1 to 5.

- Patience
- Plan the following
- Impulse control
- Risk management
- Emotional recovery

Score yourself out of a total of 25. No Judgement. Just awareness.

Ask yourself: What got better this week? What slipped?

4. The Loss Recovery Protocol

This one is close to my heart as it has saved me from emotional trauma after a major loss.

After a loss, especially a big one, follow this.

- Step away from your screen for 5 to 15 minutes. (The time will depend on the timeframe that you trade. For a swing trader/positional trader, you can take a day off.
- Take a few deep breaths.
- Ask yourself, was this loss part of my process or my emotion?
- Write down 2 lines on what you learned.
- Only resume trading if you are emotionally calm.
- The majority of us will not be calm and will want to fight back, take revenge trades, and earn back the money. So, when you do that, you will fail in the tool number 1, the 5-step trade entry pause. This continuous self-assessment saves you big time.

This tool is not about money. It is about self-control.

5. If–Then Mental Rules

This is how you rewire your instincts. Write down your rules like below.

"If I feel _____, I will do _____ instead."

Examples

- If I feel the urge to overtrade, I will close the screen for 15 minutes.
- If I miss a breakout, I will remind myself: "There is always another trade."

Keep your list short but real and write what matters to you.

Pick 2 of these tools and use them for 7 days straight. You will notice your trading feels steadier. You will still feel emotion, but you will start to act with intention.

CHAPTER 22

THE 90-DAY MENTAL FITNESS PLAN - ONE STAGE AT A TIME

"You do not have to conquer the 90 days today. You just have to conquer one day at a time."

– anonymous

22.1 Why Break It into Stages?

If you are like me and most other human beings, 90 days can sound very difficult and intimidating at first.

We live in the era of social media and instant gratification. We are bombarded with reels, instant updates, and quick rewards. The mind craves quick victories.

And that's ok. I have designed the program to instill discipline and make the outcome achievable and rewarding.

So instead of thinking of the next 90 days, I want you to think about winning three simple 30-day battles while focusing only on the immediate one day.

Each one is a victory. Each day moves you closer to building a mind you can trust under pressure.

22.2 Your Mental Fitness Journey: 3 Wins in 90 Days

Stage 1: Days 1 to 30 – Awareness and Emotional Reset

These 30 days are all about understanding yourself. Please do not rush this stage. You will be surprised to see the results if you go through this phase completely. Otherwise, the results will be very superficial, and you will continue the blame game for your losses.

Focus on:

- Catching distorted thoughts.
- Recognizing emotional spikes.
- Slow down impulsive reactions.

Tools you will use:

- The Thought Catcher
- The Reality Anchor
- The 5-Step Trade Entry Pause
- Behavioral scorecard

You Goal:

- Notice your mind working without judgement.
- Start building the muscle of observation over reaction.

Stage 2: Days 31 to 60 – Emotional Regulation and Behavior Control

You will continue to do the stage 1 activities, which are important to you and add on the below. With time, these activities hardly take a few minutes of your time.

Focus on:

- Actively reframing distorted thoughts.

- Reset emotions before action.
- Adjust risk and patience based on internal weather.

Tools you will use:

- The Belief Challenger
- The Emotional Reset Button
- The Risk Radar
- The Patience Timer
- Daily Bias Reflection
- Behavioral Scorecard
- Loss Recovery Protocol

Your Goal:

- Stop letting emotions silently control your trades.
- Build emotional separation from every trade's outcome.

Stage 3: Days 61 to 90 – Identity Strengthening and Mastery

You will continue to do the Stage 1 and 2 activities, which are important to you, and add on the below. With time, these activities hardly take a few minutes of your time.

Focus on:

- Integrating emotional resilience naturally.
- Strengthen self-trust after mistakes.
- Use Gratitude and Reflection to foster growth.

Tools you will use:

- The Confidence Builder
- The Focus Filter
- The Gratitude Journal

- Loss Recovery Protocol
- If–Then Mental Rules

You Goal:

- Trade from a place of inner strength, not fear or approval seeking.
- Redefine success as emotional mastery, not just profits.
- Set a specific outcome goal, not money but behavior – "This week, I will follow my plan 100%, regardless of the outcome."

22.3 Why This Works

By breaking the journey into three clear wins, you create:

Benefit	Why it Matters
Quick momentum	"I am succeeding already.", "I am changing already."
Emotional anchoring	"I don't need to be perfect – just present. And follow my plan."
Sustainable transformation	"I am rewiring daily habits. This is a long-term process and I am not hoping for miracles."

Each 30 days builds psychological muscle. By 90 days, you won't just have new habits, but you will have a new identity.

22.4 Traders' Mental Fitness Journey: 90 Days —— 3 Wins

Stage	Focus	Tools
Days 1 to 30	Awareness and Emotional Reset	Thought Catcher, Reality Anchor, The 5-Step Trade Entry Pause, Behavioral Scorecard
Days 31 to 60	Emotional Regulation and Behavioral Control	Belief Challenger, Emotional Reset Button, Risk Radar, Patience Timer, Daily Bias Reflection, Behavioral Score Card, Loss Recovery Protocol
Days 61 to 90	Identity Strengthening and Mastery	Confidence Builder, Focus Filter, Gratitude Journal, Loss Recovery Protocol, If–Then Rules

Progression, not perfection, where strength is built quietly but permanently.

Focus on today. Focus on the next 30 days. The journey will take care of itself. You are very close to becoming the best version of yourself.

CHAPTER 23

MY 90-DAY TRANSFORMATION: A PERSONAL JOURNEY

> *"The breakthrough didn't come from winning trades — it came from breaking the bias within me."*
>
> **– TraderPsyche**

When I created the 90-Day Mental Fitness Plan, I didn't build it for others – I built it for myself.

The inspiration came from watching my son, who was on the "healthier" side, commit to a gym routine. I had pushed him to go consistently, and to my surprise, the transformation was unbelievable. He dropped his fat percentage significantly and now trains for MMA (Mixed Martial Arts).

That visual change – the discipline, the consistency, the strength – made me think: **Why should building mental strength be any different?**

Just like the gym, mental fitness requires you to **stop doing what harms you** and **start building habits that help**. If your trading is breaking down due to emotions, fear, ego, or irrational thinking, you can't expect to change it by watching more charts. You need to train your mind, like an athlete trains their body.

So, I made a decision.

I gave myself 90 days, not to be perfect, but to become better.

To observe myself honestly. To confront my patterns. To rebuild my mindset, not around hope or motivation, but around discipline and self-awareness.

What happened next changed everything.

Days 1 to 30 – Awareness and Emotional Reset

Here, my goal was to be brutally honest with myself. I was simply trying to notice, but not in a self-critical way. I used tools like:

- Thought Catcher – To write down recurring negative self-talk and irrational thoughts.
- Reality Anchor – A small exercise that reminded me to respond to facts, not fears.
- The 5-Step Trade Entry Pause – probably the most impactful habit I developed.
- Behavioral Scorecard – A simple weekly tracker that showed me where I slipped and where I held strong.

These 30 days were like holding a mirror to my mind, and I began seeing patterns that I hadn't seen in years.

Days 31 to 60 – Emotional Regulation and Behavioral Control

I was self-aware by this stage, and it was time to act. In this phase, I used tools to respond instead of reacting and didn't try to be perfect. I relied on:

- Belief Challenger – A tool I used to question the beliefs I had about the market and myself as a trader.
- Emotional Reset button – A ritual I created to mentally reset myself after big moves.
- Risk Radar – A scan to check whether I will be able to handle the risk emotionally and financially in the trade.

- Patience Timer – Yes. I have used a timer to make me sit out and wait for quality setups.
- Daily Bias Reflection – The most eye-opening 3 min task of my day. Gave me great insight about myself.
- Loss Recovery Protocol – My go-to routine after a losing trade
- Behavioral Scorecard – Still running most weeks, giving me a good idea of my mental status.

This stage made me realize that, along with awareness, I had to control my responses and behavior. That's what helps you achieve a better trading mentality.

Days 61-90 – Identity Strengthening and Mastery

This final phase was the most powerful. I wasn't chasing discipline anymore. I was building a new identity, one that aligned with the trader I wanted to become.

Here is what helped in the final stretch:

- Confidence Builder – Helped me reinforce my strengths and stop fixating on what went wrong.
- Focus Filter – Allowed me to eliminate noise and cut down decision fatigue.
- Gratitude Journal – Kept me grounded, especially when the market tried to mess with my head.
- Loss Recovery Protocol – Continued to be my reset key.
- If-Then Rules – Simple rules that protected me from old patterns.

This phase felt like less effort and more in alignment with self. But if you think this entire journey was a walkover, it will be far from the truth.

The initial days were filled with the struggle to implement my knowledge. I have covered my experience of passing through the plan myself below, describing what I felt through each phase.

Week 1: Facing the Truth

The first week hit me hard. I began journaling my trades and emotions every day, as per the plan. I realized how much of my trading wasn't driven by logic, but by mood, bias, and ego.

There were times I struggled to write the truth – like when I overtraded or broke rules out of frustration. That's when the real work started. The discomfort felt like workout pain, but I kept showing up.

Weeks 2–3: Facing the Triggers

Around the second week, I had a good winning streak, and I felt invincible. But the plan had taught me what to watch for. I saw my risk increasing, my patience decreasing.

So, I paused.

The REBT ABCDE worksheet became my weapon. I challenged the thought: "I must capitalize now or I'm wasting this streak."

The replacement thought: "I prefer to win, but I don't have to rush. Trading isn't going anywhere."

This one belief change saved me from a potential spiral.

Weeks 4–6: Internal Resistance

This was a tough stretch. I started getting lazy. I would delay journaling. Skip affirmations. Rationalize revenge trades.

But here's the thing: because I was on the plan, I *noticed* it. Awareness is power. I didn't win every day, but I didn't spiral like before.

Instead of perfection, I focused on *consistency*. Even 70% adherence was better than my previous 10% self-discipline.

Week 7: One Trade That Changed Me

There was one trade in a small-cap stock. Beautiful setup. All signals are green.

But emotionally, I was unsettled that day due to a personal issue. My checklist had an item: *"Are you emotionally ready?"* I had to mark "No."

I didn't take the trade.

It failed.

And I felt powerful, not because I avoided a loss, but because I chose *mind over impulse*.

Week 8–9: A New Rhythm

By now, journaling wasn't a chore. It was clarity.

The mental triggers still came – greed, fear, FOMO – but they no longer hijacked me. I would acknowledge the emotion, trace the thought, and ask: "Is this 100% true?"

CBT and REBT principles became second nature.

My trades improved as I started trading and investing in time frames that suited me. But more than that, **my emotional recovery** improved. I didn't stay stuck. I bounced back faster. My equity curve smoothed out. I wasn't chasing money. I was building a mindset.

Day 90: Looking Back

On the final day, I opened my old journal and read what I had written before the journey started. That person felt familiar, but distant.

I had grown.

I wasn't perfect. But I was no longer the same.

I was:

- More aware
- More measured
- Less reactive
- More confident in uncertainty

I wasn't relying on motivation. I had built a **mental structure**.

That's what this 90-day journey did. It gave me back control over the only thing I can truly manage in trading: **myself**.

And now, if you're reading this before starting your own 90 days, here's my honest advice:

Start. Don't wait for a perfect market. Don't wait for a low-stress life.

Start where you are.

You won't be perfect. You don't need to be. Just stay consistent.

You'll look back, 90 days later, and realize: *you didn't just become a better trader – you became a stronger person.*

And that, my friend, is the real edge.

CHAPTER 24

MISTAKES I MADE WHILE FIXING MY TRADING PSYCHOLOGY

"The more decisions you make, the higher the chances are that you will make a poor decision."

– Lou Simpson

24.1 Why I am Sharing My Mistakes

When I first realized that my biggest trading problems weren't on the charts, but inside my mind, I felt a lot of excitement. I felt it would save me if I fixed it quickly.

But what happened next?

I made mistake after mistake in how I approached my mind.

- Mistakes that set me back by months.
- Mistakes that hurt more than losses.
- Mistakes that nearly made me give up trading altogether.

I don't want you to repeat them.

So let me be blunt and honest about the road I took, so that you can build yours better.

24.2 Mistake 1: Believing Awareness was Enough

Once I learned about concepts like loss aversion, emotional reasoning, and biases, I felt smart.

I thought: "Now that I know these biases exist, I won't fall into them."

But knowing is not immunity.

- I still exited good trades out of fear.
- I still chased trades out of greed.
- I still froze in the face of uncertainty.

Just because you can name a bias or distortion doesn't mean you have overcome it.

Real change began only when I started practicing catching and questioning these thoughts every single day. Not just understanding them intellectually.

24.3 Mistake 2: Trying to "Eliminate" My Emotions

For a long time, I had this fantasy:

- "If I master mindset, I will never feel fear again."
- "If I train enough, biases and distortions will vanish."

But then these emotions and feelings still came and made me think that "I am not good enough.", "I am weak."

It took me years to understand and accept that:

- Fear is a part of me and my trading.
- Doubt is a part of me and my trading.
- Greed comes out whenever I am profitable.

And to be successful, I do not need to be emotionless, I need to be resilient to these emotions. That shift changed everything.

24.4 Mistake 3: Only Working on My Mindset After a Loss

I used to awaken emotionally and internally only:

- After blowing a trade.
- After a massive emotional breakdown.
- After a humiliating revenge–trade session.

When things were going well, my discipline would come off and my mind would say, **"I am doing well now. No need for mindset work today."**

Big Mistake. Strength is built when you don't need it, so that you can use it when you do.

Mental fitness is like any other routine. You build it daily, not just in an emergency.

24.5 Mistake 4: Expecting Linear Emotional Growth

I thought "I have learned all possible psychological concepts and now things would be great for me every week. I felt every week I would be calmer and every month I would be more confident.

Reality?

Progress was chaotic.

Some days, I was unstoppable. Some days I felt like starting over again.

Sometimes after a big win, I would fall into self-sabotage faster than ever. Sometimes after a bad week, I would show more patience than I thought possible.

Growth was not linear. It was layered, messy, but beautiful once I accepted it.

24.6 Mistake 5: Thinking Psychology Alone Would Save Me.

Let me explain this by comparing it with my stint in Chess. I was a national level chess player in the sub-junior category in India. There are two aspects to chess, as far as I know. One is finding the next best move, combination, tactics etc., and the other is becoming mentally strong to be resilient to emotions which come out before, between, and after major tournaments.

As a player, I need to improve my game by improving in tactics, Openings, Middle Game, End Game, strategy, etc. There is no escape from that fact, and however much I improve my mental strength, without the skill, I will never win.

Coming back to trading, I used to fantasize that just by improving my trading psychology, somehow magically my edge on the market would improve. It doesn't. Both need to go together.

- Mindset magnifies good systems.
- It cannot rescue bad systems.

You will need structure, setups, risk management, and then psychology protects all of it under emotional pressure.

24.7 If You See Yourself in My Mistakes – It's a Good Sign

It means you are human. It means you are aware. It means you are already ahead of many of the traders who are still blind.

Awareness won't make your journey perfect. But it makes it possible and gives you a destination to reach.

If you can:

- Accept that emotions will show up in trading.
- Keep training your mind even on good days.
- Embrace the messy zig-zag path of growth.
- Balance emotional strength with trading structure

Then you are already doing the real work. And if you stay with it, through the struggles, the doubts, the silent emotional storms, you won't just become a better trader.

You will become a stronger, clearer, wiser version of yourself.

Trade by trade.

Day by day.

Belief by belief.

I am walking this path too, and you are not alone.

CHAPTER

25

CONCLUSION: MASTERING YOUR TRADING PSYCHOLOGY

> "The Goal of a successful trader is to make the best trades. Money is secondary."
>
> – **Alexander Elder**

25.1 Where you started

When you picked up, maybe you were frustrated, confused, and angry at yourself. Or worn down by the endless emotional storms trading throws at all of us.

Maybe you thought:

- "Maybe if I just fix my mindset, I will finally become profitable."
- "Maybe there is a trick to controlling my emotions once and for all."

What you have hopefully discovered now is deeper and much more important.

You understand that:

- You don't control emotions by force.

- You don't eliminate fear and greed.
- You don't become immune to bias or distortions.

Instead, you become **aware**. You **catch** the distortions early. You **challenge** the old beliefs that no longer serve you.

You **act** not from fear but from clarity.

You grow, trade by trade, thought by thought, reset by reset.

25.2 What This Book Has Given You

- You are aware of the psychological battlefield you walk into every single trading day.
- You understand the cognitive biases and emotional distortions that silently destroy performance.
- You know about the tools from CBT, REBT, and my real trading scars on how to catch, challenge, and reframe destructive patterns.
- You have a practical 90-Day Mental Fitness Plan, broken into achievable 30 – Day wins, to rebuild the very foundation you trade from.

And most importantly: A new identity.

The beginning of becoming your own trading psychologist. Not depending on someone else to save you. Not waiting for the market to behave. Not blaming the system, the news, or the economy.

Finally, you own your Mind, own your Growth, and you will own your Future.

25.3 What Mastering Your Own Trading Psychology Really Means

It doesn't mean you will never struggle. It means when you struggle, you will know how to respond.

It doesn't mean that you will not feel fear. It means when fear shows up, you will not obey it blindly.

It doesn't mean you will never lose trades, but you will never sabotage your account and, in the process, lose yourself.

- You will become the observer of your thoughts.
- You will become the coach who catches negative thoughts early.
- You will become the calm anchor when emotions surge.
- You will become the architect of your mind.

25.4 What I want you to remember the most

You don't have to be perfect to be powerful.

You don't have to be emotionless to be consistent.

You don't have to be fearless to be free.

Stay committed to the journey – show up consistently, pay attention to the details, make those necessary tweaks, and celebrate every little victory within yourself. Each step forward matters!

Over time, these small wins compound into something extraordinary:

- A mind that no longer crumbles when market volatility hits the roof.
- A trader who acts from processes, not panic.
- A life where growth becomes inevitable, because resilience is a part of you.

You have the tools now, the path now, and the awareness now. The next chapter isn't in this book.

It is on your next trading day. Your next emotional test, your next choice to respond differently.

This time, you won't be just trading the setups. You will be trading your growth. And that is the real trade that will change your life.

I believe in you. Now it's time for you to start believing in yourself.

A note for Systematic and Algorithmic Traders

While much of this book is directed towards discretionary traders like me, those of us who make active decisions in real time, the truth is that system and algorithmic trading is not entirely immune to psychological biases.

They too go through many psychological issues like:

- Doubting your system after a string of losses.
- Overriding automation out of fear of frustration.
- Constantly tweaking parameters, searching for "perfect" results.
- Abandoning long-term strategies because of immediate emotional discomfort.

Even when the rules are written, even when the codes are clean, the mind running the systems still matters.

Whether you trade manually or manage algorithms, your emotional resilience, your ability to tolerate uncertainty, and your patience to trust your edge all remain the foundation for long-term success.

The market tests not just your strategy, but your ability to trust the process you built. In that way discretionary or systematic, we all are facing similar inner battles.

And with the right tools, we can all win them.

SECTION 6
BONUS SECTION

CHAPTER 26

TRADERPSYCHE SELF-TRANSFORMATION MINI WORKBOOK

> "Real change doesn't happen from reading alone. It happens when you reflect, apply, and rebuild – thought by thought."
>
> — anonymous

Part 1: TraderPsyche – Self-Reflection Quiz

"Every distorted thought you catch is one step closer to clarity."

Instructions:

- Mark each statement that you feel applies to you while trading or investing.
- Be honest. There are no right or wrong answers. Only insights.

The Questions

1. I feel personally attacked when a trade goes wrong.
2. I often find it hard to let go of a stock once I've invested in it, even if it's falling.
3. I search for news that supports the position I am already holding.
4. After two or three losses, I doubt my entire trading system.

5. I believe if I lose one trade, I am likely to lose the next one too.
6. I feel uncomfortable exiting a profitable trade even when my plan says to.
7. I keep adjusting my stop loss wider to avoid feeling "wrong."
8. I think "the market is unfair" when my setups don't work.
9. I feel an urgent need to act after seeing others talk about a stock/index.
10. I often think in extreme terms – "either I'm a successful trader or a complete failure."
11. I enter trades larger than usual after a big win, feeling unstoppable.
12. I feel ashamed to show my losing trades to anyone.
13. I find myself regretting "missed opportunities" days after they happened.
14. I avoid trading after a loss out of fear of being wrong again.
15. I jump into revenge trades trying to recover losses quickly.
16. I find it difficult to trust a system unless it wins almost all the time.
17. I attribute my winners to skill, but my losers to bad luck.
18. I often think, "This loss proves I'm not good enough."
19. I set unrealistically high expectations from single trades.
20. I find myself needing external validation about my trading decisions (friends, forums, experts).

How to Use this Quiz?

- No Judgement
- If you recognize yourself in many statements, congratulations – you are becoming self-aware.
- Pick 1-2 biases/distortions you feel most often, and use the tools from the toolbox and 90-Day plan to work on them specifically.
- Compare your answers with Bias and Distortion Interpretation Table.

Part 2: Bias and Distortion Interpretation Table

Question	Bias/Distortion	Explanation
1	Labeling, All-or-Nothing Thinking.	Associating a single trade's outcome leading to self-judgement.
2	Endowment Effect, Loss Aversion	Overvaluing owned assets and fearing losses more than valuing gains.
3	Confirmation Bias	Seeking information that confirms existing beliefs, ignoring contradicting data.
4	Overgeneralization	Drawing broad conclusions from a few events, leading to unnecessary system changes.
5	Gamblers Fallacy	Expecting future outcomes to be influenced by past events in independent scenarios.
6	Loss Aversion, Overconfidence bias	Fear of missing out on additional gains, leading to deviation from the plan.
7	Loss Aversion, Endowment Effect	Avoiding the realization of losses and overvaluing current positions.
8	Emotional Reasoning	Letting emotions dictate perceptions of fairness, rather than objective analysis.
9	Herd Mentality	Following the crowd without independent analysis, driven by fear of missing out.

10	All-or-Nothing Thinking	Viewing situations in black and white terms, ignoring the spectrum of outcomes.
11	Overconfidence Bias	Overestimating abilities after success, leading to riskier decisions.
12	Labeling	Associating losses with personal failure, leading to shame and secrecy.
13	Emotional Reasoning	Allowing emotions to dominate thoughts about past decisions, hindering progress.
14	Catastrophizing	Anticipating the worst possible outcome leads to avoidance behavior.
15	Loss Aversion, Emotional Reasoning	Making impulsive decisions driven by the desire to offset negative emotions.
16	Perfectionism, All-or-Nothing Thinking	Expecting flawless performance leading to unrealistic standards.
17	Self-serving Bias	Taking credit for successes while deflecting blame for failures.
18	Labeling, All-or-Nothing Thinking	Defining self-worth based on individual outcomes, ignoring overall performance.
19	Overconfidence Bias	Overestimating abilities on a single trade
20	Confirmation Bias	Relying on others' opinions to validate decisions, undermining self-confidence.

Part 3: TraderPsyche – Self-Reflection Worksheet

"Awareness without action changes nothing. Awareness with action changes everything."

How to Use This Worksheet:

- After completing the 20-Question Self-Reflection Quiz.
- Refer to the Biases and Distortions you most recognize yourself in.
- Use this sheet to create your first action plan for mental mastery.

Step 1: Identify your Top Biases/Distortions

Instructions:

Pick two biases or distortions you feel are most sabotaging your trading day.

Bias/Distortion	My Real Life Examples (Briefly describe a situation where you experienced this)
Bias/Distortion 1	
Bias/Distortion 2	

Step 2: Analyze the Emotional Triggers

Instructions:

Reflect on what usually triggers these biases.

Bias/Distortion	Common Emotional Trigger
Bias/Distortion 1	Fear of loss? Fear of missing out? Need to prove something?
Bias/Distortion 2	Impatience? Self-doubt? External noise?

Step 3: Apply Tools from Traders Mental Toolbox
Instructions:

Bias/Distortion	Tool I Will Use	How I Will Apply it
Bias/Distortion 1	(eg: Thought Catcher)	(eg: I will write down my automatic thoughts)
Bias/Distortion 2	(eg: Belief Challenger)	(eg: Write down the irrational belief and challenge it with facts.)

Step 4: Design a Mini 7-Day Challenge
Instructions:

Create a simple, practical 7-day emotional fitness challenge for yourself.

Question	Your Action
Which two emotional habits will I track daily?	(e.g.: Exiting on plan, not chasing news.)
How will I measure my emotional responses?	(e.g.: journal 2 lines after every trading session.)
What reward will I give myself for completing 7 days?	(e.g.: A day off from charts, a small treat. Something which you enjoy.)

Final Reminder

- You don't need to fix everything at once.
- Small emotional wins, repeated daily, will build true psychological mastery.
- Be patient, be honest, and be kind to yourself.

The markets test your strategy. But your growth will come from how you rebuild your mind.

Part 4: 90-Day Mental Fitness Tracker

You have your 90-Day Mental Fitness Plan, a clear path to rebuilding your trading mind, one stage at a time. But having a path and walking the path are two different things.

Growth doesn't come just from reading about tools.

- It comes from the hard work you do daily.
- From tracking your reactions,
- From seeing your mind shift one small decision at a time.

That's where the 90-Day Mental Fitness Tracker comes in.

This is your mirror. This is your accountability partner. This is the silent journal where you will see your real transformation take shape, not through giant leaps but through small, consistent emotional victories.

Each day you will fill in at least one line honestly, and you will be upgrading your trading mind bit by bit.

You don't need to be perfect. You just need to stay aware, stay honest, and be consistent.

Let's begin the real work – one day at a time.

"You don't build a stronger mind overnight. You build it one thought, one decision, one emotional reset at a time."

How to Use This Tracker:

- Each day, take 2-3 minutes after your trading or investing session.
- Fill in these simple checkpoints honestly without any self-judgment.
- Focus on progress, not perfection.

- Small daily wins will compound into emotional resilience over the next 90 days.

Mental Fitness Journey Breakdown – We have already covered

Stage	Focus	Tools
Days 1 to 30	Awareness and Emotional Reset	Thought Catcher, Reality Anchor, The 5-Step Trade Entry Pause, Behavioral Scorecard
Days 31 to 60	Emotional Regulation and Behavioral Control	Belief Challenger, Emotional Reset Button, Risk Radar, Patience Timer, Daily Bias Reflection, Behavioral Score Card, Loss Recovery Protocol
Days 61 to 90	Identity Strengthening and Mastery	Confidence Builder, Focus Filter, Gratitude Journal, Loss Recovery Protocol, If–Then Rules

- Each 30 days has a clear psychological focus.
- You are building mental muscles progressively, just like physical training.

Now, let us go through the Daily Mental Fitness log template to do the daily work.

Daily Mental Fitness Log Template (You can make this table in a Notebook or Excel Worksheet.) It is not necessary that you only use one tool on each day. You might use more than one tool but add your experience for each on the tracker for your review later.

Day	Date	Emotional Awareness (Yes/No)	Mental Tool Used Today (e.g. Thought Catcher)	1-Sentence Reflection
1			The Thought Catcher	
2			The Reality Anchor	
...				
30				Stage 1 Complete.
31	(Start Stage 2)			
...				
60				Stage 2 Complete.
61	(Start Stage 3)			
90				90-Day Journey complete.

Very Important to understand that there will be some days:
- When you will forget to fill this.
- When you will not feel proud of what you write.

- When the losses will be so large that you will not even want to open this sheet.

That is normal. The real transformation comes from **showing up**. Not from perfection.

You are not just tracking your trades. You are now tracking the mind that trades. And that is where real mastery begins.

Part 5: 10 Daily Affirmations for Traders

Every morning, before the charts and news,
Every evening, after the trades,
Every time you feel emotional turmoil rising.

Breathe. Center yourself and remind yourself who you are building yourself to be.

10 Daily Affirmations

1. "I am a work in progress, and that progress is enough for today."
2. "I allow my emotions to visit. But I don't let them drive my decisions."
3. "I respect my trading plan more than I chase feelings."
4. "Every trade is a new opportunity to practice discipline, not perfection."
5. "Losses do not define me. How I respond to losses does."
6. "My worth is not measured by my last trade, but by my long-term growth."
7. "I trust my preparation, even when self-doubt creeps in."
8. "Mistakes are part of mastery. Today's error is tomorrow's upgrade."
9. "I prefer to win, but I accept that survival and learning are bigger victories."

10. "The market doesn't control my mind. I choose how I interpret and respond, always."

How to Use these Affirmations?

- Pick 2 to 3 each day that resonate most with where you are emotionally.
- Recite them aloud slowly, not like a chant but like a truth you are stepping into.
- Feel their meaning, imagine yourself already believing in them.
- Adjust them over time, if you find better words that suit your personal journey.
- Write your favorite one each week on a sticky note where you can see it before trading.

These aren't magic spells. **They are emotional reminders that you are always bigger than a single trade, day, or emotion.**

The mind you train today becomes the trader you trust tomorrow. Train it well.

ACKNOWLEDGEMENTS

As I sit here reflecting on this journey of trading, of rebuilding, of writing, I realize none of it would have been possible alone.

I offer my deepest gratitude:

To my Amma,

whose unconditional love, prayers, and belief in me never wavered even when I stopped believing in myself. Your strength motivates me, and this book carries your spirit.

To Ritu, my wife,

For standing through the storms, not just financial ones, but the emotional ones few ever see. For believing in my growth when all I could see were my failures. This book is as much yours as it is mine.

To Anjali and Aditya,

Thanks for fixing my typos, catching my grammar crimes, and surviving my stress storms. This book's cleaner and I'm calmer because of you.

To the trading community,

Especially those who are struggling, this book is for you. For every silent battle you fight in your mind. For every day you choose to stand up again and face the uncertainty. You are stronger than you realize.

Acknowledgements

To Yeshwant Rao,

Who introduced me to the fascinating, frustrating, beautiful language of technical analysis. Your teachings lit the first spark, a spark that grew into a lifelong journey of learning, losing, winning, and evolving.

To Dr Aaron T Beck and Dr Albert Ellis

Whose pioneering work in Cognitive Behavioral Therapy (CBT) and Rational Emotive Behavior Therapy (REBT) gave me and millions of others a path to understand, challenge, and change the deepest parts of ourselves. Your insights save not just trades but lives.

Every chapter of this book, every tool, every reflection carries pieces of all of you. Thank you for walking this unseen journey with me.

ABOUT THE AUTHOR

Anand Siva Kumar

Trader, Risk Manager, Student of the Mind.

Anand's trading journey spans over 16 years, a path carved through Indian Equities, futures and options, and international crude oil markets.

He knows firsthand the highs of market wins and the humbling, painful lessons of losses.

Before focusing full-time on markets, Anand held senior Trading & Risk Management positions at Reliance Industries Limited and Essar Oil UK Limited. He has a Bachelor's degree in Chemical Engineering and is pursuing postgraduate studies in Clinical Psychology, combining engineering logic with insights into human behavior.

Anand is a CMT (Chartered Market Technician), ERP (Energy Risk Professional) and EPAT (Executive Programme in Algorithmic Trading) certificate holder, reflecting his deep technical understanding of markets and risk.

He is also a certified CBT (Cognitive Behavioral Therapy) Practitioner, with additional training in REBT (Rational Emotive Behavior Therapy), specializing in applying psychological tools to trading and investment behavior.

But titles and certificates only tell part of the story.

About the Author

Anand's real education came from the markets themselves- from blowing up accounts, struggling through emotional sabotage, facing depression and anxiety and ultimately rebuilding both his trading strategies and trading mind.

This book was born from his belief that success in trading is not just about mastering the charts, but it's also about mastering yourself. And that anyone willing to confront their inner patterns honestly, patiently, and persistently can transform their journey. Not just as a trader but also as a person.

Through this work, Anand hopes to offer every struggling trader a rare combination:

- Psychological insight.
- Practical tools.
- And most importantly – real empathy.

Because he has been where you are and he knows that with the right tools and enough inner work, you can become who you were meant to be.

FURTHER READING AND REFERENCES

To every trader seeking clarity, mental resilience, and self-mastery, the following books and resources have inspired, guided, and supported many of the psychological principles explored in *TraderPsyche: From Bias to Breakthrough*. These are recommended for those who wish to dive deeper into trading psychology, cognitive behavior, and emotional regulation.

Cognitive Behavioral Therapy (CBT) & Rational Emotive Behavior Therapy (REBT)

1. *Feeling Good: The New Mood Therapy* **by Dr. David D. Burns**
   A timeless classic introducing CBT techniques to challenge negative thinking and reshape your emotional responses.
2. *A Guide to Rational Living* **by Dr. Albert Ellis and Dr. Robert A. Harper**
   A foundational work in REBT that teaches how to identify and defeat self-defeating beliefs and rigid demands.
3. *Cognitive Therapy and the Emotional Disorders* **by Dr. Aaron T. Beck**
   The seminal book that introduced the core framework of CBT focuses on distorted thinking patterns and emotional change.

   Trading Psychology and Performance
4. *Trading in the Zone* **by Mark Douglas**
   A modern classic that explores the mindset required for trading consistency, detachment, and mental clarity.

5. *The Daily Trading Coach: 101 Lessons for Becoming Your Own Trading Psychologist* **by Dr. Brett N. Steenbarger**
   An excellent manual offering daily exercises and psychological tools to improve trader's mindset.
6. *Enhancing Trader Performance* **by Dr. Brett N. Steenbarger**
   Combining elite performance coaching with trading to help traders achieve long-term improvement.
7. *The Psychology of Trading* **by Dr. Brett N. Steenbarger**
   Real-life stories and clinical insights that highlight the emotional and mental struggles traders face.

   Cognitive Biases and Behavioral Finance
8. *Thinking, Fast and Slow* **by Daniel Kahneman**
   A groundbreaking work on how human decision-making is affected by cognitive biases – highly relevant for traders.
9. *Misbehaving: The Making of Behavioral Economics* **by Richard H. Thaler**
   Blends storytelling and research to show how real-world decision-making differs from theoretical models.